After
Prohibition

After Prohibition

AN ADULT APPROACH TO DRUG POLICIES IN THE 21ST CENTURY

edited by

Timothy Lynch

CATO INSTITUTE
Washington, D.C.

Library of Congress Cataloging-in-Publication Data

After Prohibition : an adult approach to drug policies in the 21st century /
  edited by Timothy Lynch.
     p. cm.
  Includes bibliographical references and index.
  ISBN 1-882577-93-0 (cloth) — ISBN 1-882577-94-9 (pbk.)
  1. Drug abuse—Government policy—United States. 2. Narcotics,
Control of—United States. 3. Narcotics and crime—United States.
4. Drug legalization—United States. 5. United States—Politics and
government. 6. United States—Foreign relations. I. Lynch, Timothy.
HV5825.A669   2000
362.29'0973'09051—dc21   00-047437

Printed in the United States of America.

CATO INSTITUTE
1000 Massachusetts Ave., N.W.
Washington, D.C. 20001

Contents

Foreword

This book contains revised versions of papers given at a conference on "Beyond Prohibition: An Adult Approach to Drug Policies in the 21st Century," held at the Cato Institute on October 5, 1999. The papers presented range widely over all aspects of current drug policy. The final two chapters record a debate held at the conference on whether America should legalize drugs.

Whatever your view about that issue, I believe that you cannot read this book without recognizing the social tragedy that has resulted from the attempt to prohibit people from ingesting an arbitrary list of substances designated "illegal drugs." That list includes marijuana, for which there is no recorded case of a human death from overdose in several thousand years of use and which has important medicinal uses, but excludes alcohol, which also has important medicinal uses but for which the annual death toll in the United States alone is measured in the tens if not hundreds of thousands. Not since the collapse of the attempt to prohibit the ingestion of alcohol has our liberty been in such danger from the misnamed "war on drugs."

How can there be a war on drugs? Can there be a war on stones, on buildings, on aspirin? Surely, wars are on living, not inanimate, objects. And this war is being waged on people. Like every war, it is being waged in wanton disregard of "Life, Liberty, and the Pursuit of Happiness"—"unalienable rights" with which we are endowed by our Creator, according to the Declaration of Independence.

As a nation, we have been destroying foreign countries because we cannot enforce our own laws. As a nation, we have been responsible for the murder of literally hundreds of thousands of people at home and abroad by fighting a war that should never have been started and can be won, if at all, only by converting the United States into a police state. The annual arrest of nearly a million and a half people suspected of a drug offense, most of them for simple possession of small quantities, is frightening evidence of how far along that road we have already gone. So too is the overcrowding of our prisons, despite an unprecedented increase in capacity, leading to the release of persons convicted of violent crimes in order to make room for persons convicted of a drug offense and given minimum required sentences. Minimum required sentences that are sometimes so harsh that at least one judge has resigned rather than be the instrument for imposing cruel and inhumane punishment, and numerous other judges have registered strong protests (see chapter 8). So too is the fact, noted by Nova University law professor Steven Wisotsky, that "law enforcement officials—now joined by the military forces of the United States—have the power, with few limits, to snoop, sniff, survey, and detain, without warrant or probable cause, in the war against drug trafficking. Property may be seized on slight evidence and forfeited to the state or federal government without proof of the personal guilt of the owner. . . . [and] an increasingly imperial federal government has applied intimidating pressures to shop owners and others in the private sector to help implement federal drug policy."

Why is it that laws against the ingestion of a class of substances have proved to be so much greater a threat to our freedom than laws against theft, assault, and murder? The answer is simple. Persons who have been harmed by theft, assault, and murder have a strong incentive to report the crime to law enforcement officials. There is a clear and evident victim. Enforcement of the law is a cooperative enterprise that enlists the assistance of the persons harmed.

By contrast, when a willing seller and a willing buyer transfer a substance that has been designated illegal, no one has an incentive to report what the law in its majesty has declared a crime. No one has a direct incentive to cooperate with law enforcement officials. Evidence must be obtained in other ways, such as the use of informers—a practice that every totalitarian state has engaged in when it made it a crime to hold or publish the "wrong" beliefs, a crime that willing participants have no incentive to report. The Nazis and the Communists alike encouraged children to spy on and report their parents for "crimes against the state," and so does the U.S. Drug Enforcement Agency (see chapter 10).

The lack of anyone who has a direct incentive to report an offense is also the reason drug enforcers are driven to warrantless searches, seizures of property without due process, and all of the other violations of civil liberties that have become so common in the relentless prosecution of the drug war.

The high financial stakes enhance the danger to our liberty. They produce widespread corruption, which requires the use of ever more resources to monitor the monitors, and enable drug dealers to finance armies and arms not obviously inferior to the armies and arms of the drug warriors. Only the well-financed and well-armed drug dealers can survive, with the ironic result that our drug enforcement efforts protect the major drug cartels from competition— more effectively than the OPEC cartel was ever able to protect itself from competition!

Law enforcement agencies are major beneficiaries of the drug war at the same time that law enforcement is a major victim. The agencies benefit from the many billions of dollars spent on pursuing the drug war and from the proceeds of forfeiture, an increasingly attractive and lucrative source of funds. Law enforcement suffers because the attempt to enforce laws against victimless crime breaks the link between law enforcers and the community; widespread corruption engendered by the vast sums at stake destroys the trust between police and public that is essential for the proper enforcement of the law (see chapter 7). Moreover, though total expenditures on law enforcement has increased greatly, so large a fraction goes to the drug war that less is available to enforce the laws against theft, assault and murder.

The Declaration of Independence tells us that "governments are instituted among men" in order "to secure" "certain unalienable rights," and that "whenever any form of government becomes destructive of these ends, it is the right of the people to alter or abolish it." A nanny government has become destructive of these ends. It is past time that we alter it.

Milton Friedman
Hoover Institution
Stanford, California
September 8, 2000

Acknowledgments

This book was made possible by the interest and encouragement of Cato president Edward H. Crane and executive vice president David Boaz. Other individuals to whom I am grateful include David Lampo, Cato's director of publications, who refused to let this project fall behind schedule; Adel Carlock, my assistant, who proofread the manuscript and offered helpful suggestions; and Christie Raniszewski, for all her work on the October 1999 Cato conference, "Beyond Prohibition," at which the chapters in this book were first presented.

I thank all of the contributors for their hard work in preparing these papers for publication. I especially want to thank Gov. Gary Johnson for taking a stand on this controversial subject. I suspect that many government officials believe that the drug war has failed but have elected to keep their silence rather than to take any action that could risk their sacred posts.

Last, I owe an enormous debt of gratitude to Milton Friedman, not only for his gracious contribution to this volume, but also for opening my eyes to the myriad ways in which government intervention causes more harm than good. It was a *Newsweek* column by Friedman that first piqued my intellectual interests in 1982. It is thus a distinct honor to have Friedman's participation and support for my first book.

PART I

INTRODUCTION

1. Tabula Rasa for Drug Policy

Timothy Lynch

America's drug policies are not seriously debated in Washington, D.C. Year after year, our elected representatives in Congress focus on essentially two questions: (1) How much more money should they spend on the drug war? and (2) How should they spend the money? In the months preceding elections, politicians typically try to pin the blame for the "drug problem" on one another.[1] After the election, the cycle repeats itself.

Outside of our nation's capital, however, it is apparent that there is growing unease about the war on drugs. More and more Americans are concluding that the drug war has been given a chance to work and has failed. Voters in California, Arizona, Oregon, Washington, Nevada, Alaska, and Maine have rejected the lobbying efforts of federal officials and have approved initiatives calling for the legalization of marijuana for medicinal purposes. Two sitting governors, Jesse Ventura in Minnesota and Gary Johnson in New Mexico, have now gone so far as to declare the drug war a failure. As public opinion continues to turn against the war, we can expect more elected officials to speak out against the status quo.[2]

Federal officials do not yet appreciate the extent of citizens' dissatisfaction with the war on drugs. Congress continues to propose and enact laws with platitudinous titles—"The Drug-Free Families Act," "The Drug-Free School Zones Act," "Western Hemisphere Drug Elimination Act of 1998," and, most recently, believe it or not, "The Drug-Free Century Act." Not many people outside the capital

---

[1]See, for example, John Mica, "Was War on Drugs Sabotaged?" *Washington Times*, February 15, 2000; and Bill McCollum, "Waving the White Flag in Drug War?" *Washington Times*, March 10, 1998.

[2]Some politicians will undoubtedly flip-flop. See, for example, Ceci Connolly and Thomas Edsall, "Gore Backs 'Flexibility' on Medical Marijuana," *Washington Post*, December 15, 1999; and Katharine Seelye, "Gore Retreats from Earlier Signal of Support for Medical Use of Marijuana," *New York Times*, May 17, 2000.

3

are even paying attention to those laws, and few take the rhetoric seriously.

However, some people of goodwill continue to support the drug war. Their rationale is essentially this: We may not be close to achieving a "drug-free" society, but our present situation would only deteriorate if the government were to stop prosecuting the drug war. The burden of persuasion on that proposition has always rested with drug reformers. But nowadays it is a burden that the reformers happily accept as they are buoyed by the realization that the momentum in the drug policy debate is shifting in their direction.[3] Reformers are as eager as ever to debate the efficacy of the drug laws—whereas supporters of the drug war discuss the issue only grudgingly. A close examination of our experience with the war on drugs will explain why that is so.

The Case for Criminalizing Drug Use

Why should an adult man or woman be arrested, prosecuted, and imprisoned for using heroin, opium, cocaine, or marijuana? The answer, according to the most prominent supporters of the drug war, is simple: Drug use is wrong. Drug use is wrong because it is immoral and it is immoral because it degrades human beings. The prominent social scientist James Q. Wilson has articulated that view in the following terms:

> Even now, when the dangers of drug use are well under-stood, many educated people still discuss the drug problem in almost every way except the right way. They talk about the "costs" of drug use and the "socioeconomic factors" that shape that use. They rarely speak plainly—drug use is wrong because it is immoral and it is immoral because it enslaves the mind and destroys the soul.[4]

William J. Bennett, America's first drug czar, has expressed a very similar view: "A citizen in a drug-induced haze, whether on his

---

[3]The Drug Enforcement Administration has acknowledged that "the voters changed the complexion of the debate forever" by opting to liberalize the drug laws in California and Arizona on November 5, 1996. See U.S. Department of Justice, Drug Enforcement Administration, "A Police Chief's Guide to the Legalization Issue," http://www.usdoj.gov/dea/demand/policechief.htm.

[4]Quoted in William J. Bennett, John J. DiIulio, Jr., and John P. Walters, *Body Count* (New York: Simon and Schuster, 1996), pp. 140–41.

backyard deck or on a mattress in a ghetto crack house, is not what the founding fathers meant by the 'pursuit of happiness.' . . . Helpless wrecks in treatment centers, men chained by their noses to cocaine—these people are slaves."[5]

To eradicate this form of "slavery," Wilson, Bennett, and others believe the government should vigorously investigate, prosecute, and jail anyone who sells, uses, or possesses mind-altering drugs. The criminal sanction should be used "to take drug users off the streets and deter new users from becoming more deeply involved in so hazardous an activity."[6]

For more than 25 years the American political establishment has offered its unflagging support for banning drugs. In 1972 President Richard Nixon appointed Wilson chairman of the National Advisory Council for Drug Abuse Prevention. In 1973 President Nixon created the Drug Enforcement Administration, a police agency that focuses exclusively on federal drug law violations. President Ronald Reagan designated narcotics as an official threat to America's "national security." President Reagan also signed the Military Cooperation with Law Enforcement Officials Act, which authorized the military to assist federal and state police agencies in the drug war. President George Bush created the Office of National Drug Control Policy and appointed Bennett national drug czar in order to centralize control and coordinate activities of federal agencies (the Federal Bureau of Investigation, Customs, and the Coast Guard, for example) in the drug war. President Bill Clinton appointed a former military commander, General Barry McCaffrey, drug czar in 1996.

Congress has played a supporting role; since the early 1970s lawmakers have been escalating the federal government's efforts to combat drugs. To get some perspective on the steady expansion that has taken place over the years, consider these facts: In 1979 the federal government spent $900 million on various anti-drug programs; in 1989 it spent $5 billion; in 1999 it spent nearly $18 billion.[7]

---

[5]William J. Bennett, "Should Drugs Be Legalized?" *Reader's Digest*, March 1990, p. 94.

[6]William J. Bennett, "A Response to Milton Friedman," *Wall Street Journal*, September 19, 1989.

[7]For additional background on government expansion of the drug war, see Eric Blumenson and Eva Nilsen, "Policing for Profit: The Drug War's Hidden Economic Agenda," *University of Chicago Law Review* 65 (1998): 35–114.

Assessing the Drug War: Feedback from Reality

According to the Office of National Drug Control Policy, vigorous law enforcement tactics play an important role in reducing drug abuse and its consequences by doing two things:

- *Reducing demand.* By enforcing the laws against drug use, police increase social disapproval of drugs and discourage substance abuse. Moreover, arrest—and the resulting threat of imprisonment—offers a powerful incentive for many addicts to take treatment seriously.
- *Disrupting supply.* The movement of drugs from sources of supply to our nation's streets requires sophisticated organizations. When law enforcement detects and dismantles a drug ring, less heroin, cocaine, methamphetamine, and marijuana find their way to our streets. Seizures reduce availability.[8]

The billions of dollars that Congress has allocated to drug law enforcement have produced indisputable results. The criminal justice system has grown much larger—there are more police officers, prosecutors, judges, and prison guards than ever before. Moreover, the number of arrests, convictions, and prisoners and the amount of seized contraband have increased exponentially over the years. Indeed, in February 1999 the *New York Times* reported that "every 20 seconds, someone in America is arrested for a drug violation. Every week, on average, a new jail or prison is built to lock up more people in the world's largest penal system."[9]

There is much government activity—but is the Office of National Drug Control Policy achieving its twin objectives of "reducing demand" and "disrupting supply"? The demand for illegal drugs remains strong. According to the National Household Survey on Drug Abuse, 11 million Americans can be classified as "current users" (past month) of marijuana and 1.8 million Americans as current users of cocaine.[10] As startling as those numbers are, they represent only the tip of the proverbial iceberg. Millions of other individuals

---

[8]Office of National Drug Control Policy, *National Drug Control Strategy: 2000 Annual Report* (Washington: Office of National Drug Control Policy, 2000), p. 66.

[9]Timothy Egan, "War on Crack Retreats, Still Taking Prisoners," *New York Times*, February 28, 1999.

[10]Office of National Drug Control Policy, pp. 12–25. See also "Teenagers' Drug Use Rising, Survey Finds," *New York Times*, June 9, 2000.

can be classified as "occasional users," and tens of thousands of people use less-popular illicit drugs—such as heroin and methamphetamine. The government's own statistics show that millions and millions of Americans break the law every single month.

The supply of drugs has not been hampered in any serious way by the war on drugs. Perhaps the most dramatic evidence of the failure of the drug war is the flourishing open-air drug markets in Washington, D.C.—the city where the drug czar and the Drug Enforcement Administration are headquartered.[11] News reports also indicate recurring problems along both the Canadian and Mexican borders.[12] A commission on federal law enforcement practices chaired by former director of the FBI William Webster, recently offered this blunt assessment of the interdiction situation: "Despite a record number of seizures and a flood of legislation, the Commission is not aware of any evidence that the flow of narcotics into the United States has been reduced."[13]

A "Never Say Die" Mindset: Confusing Perseverance with Bullheadedness

Even though law enforcement efforts have been unable to seriously disrupt the supply of illegal drugs and the demand for narcotics, many people hesitate to draw the conclusion that the drug war has failed. That might be a reasonable conclusion for anyone who chooses to focus solely on drug use. It is lamentable that drug use and addiction rates would likely increase if the criminal sanction were lifted. However, a fair appraisal of the drug war must take all of the war's negative repercussions into account.[14] Some of the

[11]See Allan Lengel, "Struggle with a Stubborn Drug Trade: Closing D.C. Open-Air Markets Isn't Easy," *Washington Post,* January 31, 2000.

[12]See "Police Battle Booming Marijuana Industry in British Columbia," Associated Press, February 2, 2000; and Douglas Farah and Molley Moore, "2000 Miles of Disarray in Drug War: U.S.–Mexico Border Effort 'a Shambles,' " *Washington Post,* March 9, 1998.

[13]Commission on the Advancement of Federal Law Enforcement, *Law Enforcement in a New Century and a Changing World* (Washington: Commission on the Advancement of Federal Law Enforcement, 2000), p. 85.

[14]The negative repercussions are discussed in the other chapters of this volume. See also David Boaz, "A Drug-Free America—Or a Free America," *U.C. Davis Law Review* 24 (1991): 617–36; and James Ostrowski, "The Moral and Practical Case for Drug Legalization," *Hofstra Law Review* 18 (1990): 607–702.

undeniable consequences of criminalizing drug use include the following:

- The black market generates billions of dollars for gangster organizations. The criminal proceeds are often used to finance other criminal activity.[15]
- Rival gangs use violence to usurp and defend territory for drug sales. Innocent people, including children, get caught in that crossfire.[16]
- Billions of taxpayer dollars are squandered every year in a futile attempt to keep drugs from entering the country. The government cannot even keep narcotics out of its own prisons—and yet it spends millions every month trying to keep contraband from arriving by air, land, and sea.[17]
- A disturbingly large number of undesirable police practices—paramilitary raids, roadblocks, wiretapping, use of informers, property seizures—have become routine because of the difficulty of detecting drug offenses. Countless innocent people have had their phones tapped and their homes and cars searched. Some innocent bystanders have been shot; some have been killed.[18]
- Police departments from Los Angeles to Chicago to New York are reeling from corruption scandals. Police commanders say they have discovered a new breed of corrupt officers. A gen-

[15]See Commission on the Advancement of Federal Law Enforcement, p. 71; and U.S. Department of State, *International Narcotics Control Strategy Report* (Washington: U.S. Department of State, 2000), p. 41.

[16]See Michael Janofsky, "Some Midsize Cities Miss Trend As Drug Deals and Killings Soar," *New York Times,* January 15, 1998; and Pam Belluck, "Gang Gunfire May Chase Chicago Children from Their School," *New York Times,* November 17, 1997.

[17]See Paul W. Valentine, "19 Inmates Moved in Bid to Bust Drug Ring," *Washington Post,* February 14, 1999; and David Stout, "Coast Guard Using Sharpshooters to Stop Boats," *New York Times,* September 14, 1999.

[18]See Kevin Flynn, "Shooting Raises Scrutiny of Police Antidrug Effort," *New York Times,* March 25, 2000; Mark Arax, "Small Farm Town's SWAT Team Leaves a Costly Legacy," *Los Angeles Times,* April 5, 1999; Mark Babineck, "Six Officers Fired for Botched Drug Raid Shooting," Associated Press, November 3, 1998; Sam Howe Verhovek, "Pentagon Halts Drug Patrols after Border Killing," *New York Times,* July 31, 1997; and Jim McGee, "Wiretapping Rises Sharply under Clinton: Drug War Budget Increases Lead to Continuing Growth of High-Tech Surveillance," *Washington Post,* July 7, 1996.

eration ago, corrupt cops accepted bribes for agreeing to turn a blind eye to criminal activity. Today, corrupt officers are actually using their police powers of search and arrest to assist gangsters with their activities.[19]

- A criminal justice system that devotes some of its limited resources to drug offenders is necessarily distracted from investigating other criminal activity—such as murder, rape, and theft. Furthermore, in a system that has limited jail space, one of the unavoidable consequences of waging a drug war is that violent offenders will sometimes have to be released to make room for drug offenders.[20]

Unfortunately, the most prominent supporters of the drug war have refused to grapple with the grim consequences of that policy. Drug users are slaves, they retort, and drug legalization would undermine the "moral message" that drug use is wrong.[21] Bennett has gone so far as to say that alternative drug policies—such as drug decriminalization—would be tantamount to a cowardly surrender to an evil foe:

> Imagine if, in the darkest days of 1940, Winston Churchill had rallied the West by saying, "This war looks hopeless, and besides, it will cost too much. Hitler can't be *that* bad. Let's surrender and see what happens." That is essentially what we hear from the legalizers.[22]

After decades of ceaseless police work, it is safe to say that Bennett is confusing perseverance with bullheadedness. Unlike Bennett, Father John Clifton Marquis recognizes that well-meaning laws can sometimes produce horrendous and immoral consequences:

---

[19]See Todd S. Purdum, "Los Angeles Police Scandal May Soil Hundreds of Cases," *New York Times,* December 16, 1999; Todd Lighty, "Police Drug Scandal Touches Sheriff's Department," *Chicago Tribune,* March 16, 2000; Pam Belluck, "44 Officers Are Charged after Ohio Sting Operation," *New York Times,* January 22, 1998; and Karen DeYoung, "U.S. Colonel to Plead Guilty in Colombia Drug Probe," *Washington Post,* April 4, 2000.

[20]See Timothy Lynch, "All Locked Up," *Washington Post,* February 20, 2000; and David B. Kopel, "Prison Blues: How America's Foolish Sentencing Policies Endanger Public Safety," Cato Institute Policy Analysis no. 208, May 17, 1994.

[21]See, for example, James Q. Wilson, "Against the Legalization of Drugs," *Commentary,* February 1990, p. 21.

[22]Bennett, "Should Drugs Be Legalized?" p. 94. Emphasis in the original.

> Drug laws are a moral issue. Fifty years of drug legislation
> have produced the exact opposite effect of what those laws
> intended: the laws have created a tantalizingly profitable
> economic structure for marketing drugs. When law does not
> promote the common good, but in fact causes it to deterio-
> rate, the law itself becomes bad and must change . . . . Moral
> leaders have no alternative but to choose between authentic
> morality, which produces good, and cosmetic morality,
> which merely looks good. Drug laws look good! But the
> tragic flaw of cosmetic morality, like all other forms of cos-
> metics, is that it produces no change of substance . . . . Au-
> thentic moral leaders cannot afford the arrogant luxury of
> machismo, with its refusal to consider not "winning." Win-
> ning, in the case of drug abuse, is finding the direction and
> methods that provide the maximum amount of health and
> safety to the whole society without having a cure that is
> worse than the disease.[23]

Bennett's World War II imagery is misplaced. The notion that the
drug czar is somehow leading an army against an evil foe is an
example of what Marquis calls "arrogant machismo." America's
13-year experience with alcohol prohibition is a more apt analogy.
Americans rejected alcohol prohibition because experience showed
the federal liquor laws to be unenforceable and because alcohol
prohibition led to gang wars and widespread corruption. The war
on drugs has created a similar set of problems.

Tabula Rasa for Drug Policy

The most valuable lesson that can be drawn from the experience
of alcohol prohibition is that government cannot effectively engi-
neer social arrangements. Policymakers simply cannot repeal the
economic laws of supply and demand. Nor can they foresee the
unintended consequences that invariably follow federal intervention. Students of American history will someday wonder how today's lawmakers could readily admit that alcohol prohibition was a
disastrous mistake but recklessly pursue a policy of drug prohibition. Historians will look back on this period and marvel that Congress went so far as to have American military pilots flying reconnaissance missions over the jungles of South America looking for

[23]John Clifton Marquis, "Drug Laws Are Immoral," *U.S. Catholic*, May 1990, p. 14.

coca fields[24] and that the scripts of America's most popular television shows were once censored by the drug czar.[25]

The time has come to put an end to this tragic revisit of Prohibition. The time has come for a tabula rasa for drug policy in America. The issue is not whether drug use is a problem. It is. The issue is how to deal with that problem. Policymakers ought to address it in an open, honest, and mature manner. The law should treat substances such as marijuana and cocaine the same way it treats tobacco, beer, and whiskey—namely, by restricting sales to minors and jailing any user who endangers the safety of others (for example, operating an automobile while "under the influence.")[26] Education, moral suasion, and social pressure are the only appropriate ways to discourage adult drug use in a free and civil society.

[24]See Barry R. McCaffrey, "Aid Colombia: Why America Must Join in the War on Drugs," *Washington Times,* April 14, 2000; and Steven Lee Myers, "U.S. Pledges Military Cooperation to Colombia in Drug War," *New York Times,* December 1, 1998.

[25]See Marc Lacey and Bill Carter, "In Trade-Off with TV Networks, Drug Office Is Reviewing Scripts," *New York Times,* January 14, 2000.

[26]Bennett's attempt to distinguish heroin, cocaine, and marijuana from whiskey, beer, and tobacco is rather weak: "Although there are similarities between some of the dangers posed by illegal drugs and other threats—most of all alcohol consumption and cigarette smoking—and although alcohol is a recognized catalyst for crime, the harm caused by alcohol and cigarettes is, if anything, a reason not to treat illegal drugs in the same manner." Bennett, DiIulio, and Walters, p. 146.

2. It's Time to Legalize Drugs

Gary E. Johnson

I spent a half-million dollars of my own money to pursue my goal of becoming the governor of New Mexico. Let me make one point very clear: Not one person asked me to run for governor. Not one person. I introduced myself to the Republican Party just two weeks before I announced my candidacy for governor in 1994. The response that I got was, "We like you, we like what you say, but you need to understand, you'll never get elected. It's just not possible." I am not a typical politician.

I started a business in 1974 as a handyman. By 1994 my wife and I had 1,000 employees specializing in various tasks—electrical, mechanical, plumbing, and pipefitting. It was a dream come true. I did some things then that I still do today. I told the truth. I was on time. I did a little bit more for my customers than what I promised them I would do. With that formula, you can build and expand a business.

I am a competitive triathlete. This has been my hobby now for about 20 years. Going to the Ironman Triathlon is like a baseball player's opportunity to go to the World Series. It's like a football player's chance to go to the Superbowl. It's really exciting for me. I have a goal to climb Mount Everest after I leave office. I think it would be really cool to stand on top of the planet. I think that would be wonderful.

Every person needs to determine what makes his or her life work. In my particular case, I found that being as fit as I possibly can be makes my life work. You need to find out what that something is in your life—whether it's canoeing, playing chess, knitting, reading, or whatever it might be. Get more of what makes your life work, then get rid of those things that get in the way of what you want to do. In my life, I discovered that those things were tobacco and alcohol. I don't drink. I haven't had a drink in 12 years. I don't do drugs. I don't even do candy bars. Those things are a handicap. They really are.

13

I got my degree in political science at the University of New Mexico. I've always believed that life's highest calling is doing good by others. I've always believed that politics can be a way of accomplishing that. So this is something that I've always wanted to do. Now right or wrong, I never got involved in politics at an earlier level because I felt that if I did, I would somehow be indebted. I wanted to be in a position where I wasn't indebted to anyone. I wanted to get in office and do what I thought was right. That was the formula that I followed. Running for governor was something that I wanted to do, and I recognize that I have been given a wonderful opportunity to make a difference. I believe that I have made a positive difference.

When I am asked about my greatest accomplishment as governor, I respond by saying that we have taken a balanced approach to everything that needs to happen in New Mexico. We have held the line on taxes. We've actually reduced taxes, but not as much as I would like to have seen. We're building 500 miles of four-lane highway in New Mexico, effectively doubling the four-lane highways in the state. We have reduced the number of state employees by about 5 or 6 percent. I tell New Mexicans that the services of state government are more efficient because we're doing it with 1,300 fewer state employees. And whenever you save money, that's money you can spend in other areas. There are plenty of areas in government where that money can be spent.

We shifted over to managed care from the Medicaid model, and that was very significant. We had very overcrowded prisons in New Mexico. We built a couple of new prisons, and those prisons are run privately. I fought for that. The cost was two-thirds what it was costing us to do it as a state. Improving education has been a priority, but, regrettably, all I have done since I have taken office when it comes to education is put more and more money into a system that by all measurements is doing just a little bit worse from year to year. I'm afraid that that isn't just the experience of New Mexico. That is the trend nationally. So I am now pressing for school vouchers. School vouchers are something that I believe in. Bring competition to public school systems, and it will make a positive difference.

I am a cost-benefit analysis person. What's the cost and what's the benefit? A couple of things scream out as failing cost-benefit criteria. One is education. The other is the war on drugs. We are presently spending $50 billion a year on the war on drugs. I'm talking about police, courts, and jails. For all the money that we're putting into the war on drugs, it is an absolute failure. The "outrageous" hypothesis that I have been raising is that under a legalized scenario, we could actually hold drug use level or see it decline. I realize that is arguable. But with respect to drug abuse, I don't think you can argue about that. Under a legalized scenario, we would see the level of drug use remain the same or decline. And the same would happen with respect to drug abuse.

Sometimes people say to me, "Governor, I am absolutely opposed to your stand on drugs." I respond by asking them, "You're for drugs, you want to see kids use drugs?" Let me make something clear. I'm not pro-drug. I'm against drugs. Don't do drugs. Drugs are a real handicap. Don't do alcohol. Don't do tobacco. They are a real handicap.

There's another issue beyond cost-benefit criteria. Should you go to jail for using drugs? And I'm not talking about doing drugs and committing a crime or doing drugs and driving a car. Should you go to jail for simply doing drugs? I say no. I say that you shouldn't. People ask me, "What do you tell kids?" Well, you tell them the truth, that's what you tell them. You tell them that by legalizing drugs, we can control them, regulate them, and tax them. If we legalize drugs, we might have a healthier society. And you explain to them how that might take place. But you tell them that drugs are a bad choice. Don't do drugs. But if you do drugs, we're not going to throw you in jail for that.

Under a legalized scenario, I say there is going to be a whole new set of laws. Let me just mention a few of those new laws. Let's say you can't do drugs if you're under 21 years of age. You can't sell drugs to kids. I say employers should be able to discriminate against drug users. Employers should be able to conduct drug tests and they should not have to comply with the Americans With Disabilities Act. Do drugs and do crime? Make it like a gun. Enhance the penalty for the crime in the same way we do today with guns. Do drugs and drive? There should be a law similar to the law we have now for driving under the influence of alcohol.

I am proposing that we redirect the $50 billion that we're presently spending (state and federal) on the old set of laws to enforce a new set of laws. I sense a new society out there when you're talking about enforcing these new laws and enhancing the ability of law enforcement to focus on other crimes that are being committed. Police can crack down on speeding violations, burglaries, and other

15

crimes that law enforcement does not have the opportunity to enforce.

Under a legalized scenario, there will be a new set of problems. And we can all point them out. We can talk all day about the new set of problems that will accompany legalization. But I suggest to you that the new problems are going to be about half the negative consequence of what we've got today. A legalization model will be a dynamic process that will be fine-tuned as we go along.

I recall when I was in high school in 1971. An Albuquerque police officer came in, lit up some marijuana weeds and said, "If you smell this, run. This is marijuana and you need to know that if you do marijuana, we're going to catch you and we're going to put you in jail." I remember raising my hand at that time, asking, "What are you going to do, put 15 million people in jail?" The police officer said, "I don't care about that. I just care about the fact that if you do it, we're going to catch you and we're going to put you in jail." I'm afraid that prophecy may be coming true. In 1997 there were about 700,000 arrests for marijuana-related offenses.

Does anybody want to press a button that would retroactively punish the 80 million Americans who have done illegal drugs over the years? I might point out that I'm one of those individuals. In running for my first term in office, I offered up the fact that I had smoked marijuana. And the media was very quick to say, "Oh, so you experimented with marijuana?" "No," I said, "I *smoked* marijuana!" This is something that I did. I did it along with a lot of other people. I look back on it now and I view drugs as a handicap. I stopped because it was a handicap. The same with drinking and tobacco. But did my friends and I belong in jail? I don't think that we should continue to lock up Americans because of bad choices.

And what about the bad choices regarding alcohol and tobacco? I've heard people say, "Governor, you're not comparing alcohol to drugs? You're not comparing tobacco to drugs?" I say, "*Hell no!*" Alcohol killed 150,000 people last year. And I'm not talking about drinking and driving. I'm just talking about the health effects. The health effects of tobacco killed 450,000 people last year. I don't mean to be flippant, but I don't know of anybody who ever died from a marijuana overdose. I'm sure there are a few that smoked enough marijuana to probably die from it. I'm sure that that's the case. I understand that 2,000 to 3,000 people died last year from cocaine and heroin. Under a legalized scenario, theoretically speaking, those deaths go away. Those don't become accidental deaths anymore.

They become suicides, because we'd be talking about a legalized scenario where drugs will be controlled, where drugs will be taxed, where we would have education to go along with it. I want to be so bold as to say that marijuana is never going to have the devastating effects on society that alcohol has had on us.

My own informal poll among doctors is that 75 to 80 percent of people that doctors examine have health-related problems due to alcohol and tobacco. My brother is a cardio-thoracic surgeon, performing heart transplants. My brother says that 80 percent of the problems that he sees are alcohol and tobacco related. He says he sees about six people a year who have infected heart valves because of intravenous drug use, but the infection isn't from the drugs themselves. It's the dirty needles that cause the health problems.

Marijuana is said to be a gateway drug. We all know that, right? You're 85 times more likely to do cocaine if you do marijuana. I don't mean to be flippant, but 100 percent of all substance abuse starts with milk. You've heard it, but that bears repeating. My new mantra here is "Just Say Know." Just know that there are two sides to all these arguments. I think the facts boil down to drugs being a bad choice. Drugs are a handicap. But should someone go to jail for just doing drugs? That is the reality of what is happening today. I believe the time has come for that to end.

I've been talking about legalization and not decriminalization. Legalization means we educate, regulate, tax, and control the estimated $400 billion a year drug industry. That's larger than the automobile industry. Decriminalization is a muddy term. It turns its back to half the problems that we're facing—which is to get the entire economy of drugs above the line. So that's why I talk about legalization, meaning control, the ability to tax, the ability to regulate, and the ability to educate.

We need to make drugs a controlled substance just like alcohol. Perhaps we ought to let the government regulate it; let the government grow it; let the government manufacture it, distribute it, market it; and if that doesn't lead to decreased drug use, I don't know what would!

Kids today will tell you that legal prescription drugs are harder to come by than illegal drugs. Well, of course. To get legal drugs, you must walk into a pharmacy and show identification. It's the difference between a controlled substance and an illegal substance. A teenager today will tell you that a bottle of beer is harder to come by than a marijuana joint. That's where we've come to today. It's where we've come to with regard to controlling alcohol, but it shows how out of control drugs have become.

A legalization scenario isn't going to be like the end of alcohol prohibition. When Prohibition ended, there were advertisements on the radio right away that said, "Hey! Drink and be merry. It's cool." I don't see this like tobacco, where for so long we saw advertisements that said, "Hey! Smoking is good for your health." There are constitutional questions, but I envision advertising campaigns that discourage drug use. I don't see today's advertising campaigns as being honest, and that's part of the problem.

We need to have an honest educational campaign about drugs. The Partnership for a Drug Free America was bragging to me that it was responsible for the "Here's your brain, and here's your brain on drugs" ad. Well, some kids believe that, perhaps three-year-olds, maybe some nine- or ten-year-olds. But at some point, kids have friends that smoke marijuana for the first time. Like everybody else, I was also told that if you smoke marijuana, you're going to go crazy. You're going to do crime. You're going to lose your mind. Then you smoked marijuana for the first time and none of those things happened. Actually, it was kind of nice. And then you realized that they weren't telling you the truth. That's why I envision advertising that tells the truth, which says drugs are kind of nice and that's the lure of drugs. But the reality is that if you continue to do drugs, they are a real handicap.

"Drug Czar" Barry McCaffrey has made me his poster child for drug legalization. He claims that drug use has been cut in half and that we are winning the drug war. Well, let's assume that we have cut it in half. I don't buy that for a minute, but let's assume that it's true. Let's assume that drug use has, in fact, dropped in half. Well, if it has, in the late 1970s we were spending a billion dollars federally on the drug war. Today, the feds are spending $19 billion a year on the drug war. In the late 1970s, we were arresting a few hundred thousand people. Today, we're arresting 1.6 million people. Does that mean that as drug use declines (according to McCaffrey, it has declined by half) we're going to be spending $36 billion federally and that we're going to be arresting 3.2 million people annually? I mean, to follow that logic, when we're left with a few hundred users nationwide, we're going to be spending the entire gross national product on drug law enforcement!

I think it would be interesting to see some push polling done on the issue of drugs in this country. In other words, If the following is true, then how do you feel about "x"? If the following is true, how do you feel about "y"? But the questions that get asked today, I really feel like I understand the answers. People have been conditioned to believe that drugs are dangerous. The polls should ask, "Should you go to jail for just using drugs?" People overwhelmingly say no. But ask the question, "Should you go to jail for pushing drugs?" people say yes. People don't understand the profile of a pusher. Most people don't understand, as we New Mexicans do, that "mules" are carrying the drugs in. I'm talking about Mexican citizens who are paid a couple of hundred dollars to bring drugs across the border, and they don't even know who has given them the money. They just know that it's a king's ransom and that there are more than enough Mexican citizens willing to do that. The federal government is catching many of the mules, but the arrests are not making a difference in our war on drugs. We are catching some kingpins. Let's not deny that. But those that are caught, those links out of the chain, don't make any difference in the overall war on drugs.

I want to tell you a little bit about the response that I've been getting to this, the response to what I've been saying. Politically, this is a zero. This is absolutely a zero. Politically, for anybody holding office, for anybody that aspires to hold office, for anybody who's held office, or for anybody who has a job associated with politics, this is verboten. I am in the ground, and the dirt is being thrown on top of my coffin. But what I want to tell you is that among the public, this is absolutely overwhelming. I suggest to you that this is the biggest head-in-the-sand issue that exists in this country today. In New Mexico, I am being approached rapid fire with people saying "right on" with your statements regarding the war on drugs. And I want to suggest to you that it's a 97-to-3 difference among the public. This has been unbelievable. To give you one example, two elderly ladies came up to my table during dinner the other night, Gertrude and Mabel. They said, "We're teachers and we just think your school voucher idea sucks. But your position on the war on drugs . . . Right on! Right on!"

I'd like to end with my "Seven Principles of Good Government." This is something that I authored when I took office and you'll find that these principles dictate everything that I do.

1. Become reality driven. Don't kid yourself or others. Find out what's what and base your decisions and actions on that.

2. Always be honest and tell the truth. It's extremely difficult to

do any damage to anybody who is willing to tell the truth—regardless of the consequences.

3. Always do what's right and fair. Remember, the more you actually accomplish, the louder your critics become. You've got to learn to ignore your critics. You've got to continue to do what you think is right. You've got to maintain your integrity.

4. Determine your goal, develop a plan to reach that goal, and then act. Don't procrastinate.

5. Make sure everybody who ought to know what you're doing knows what you're doing. Communicate.

6. Don't hesitate to deliver bad news. There is always time to salvage things. There is always time to fix things. Henry Kissinger said that anything that can be revealed eventually should be revealed immediately.

7. Last, be willing to do whatever it takes to get your job done. If you've got a job that you don't love enough to do what it takes to get your job done, then quit and get one that you do love, and then make a difference.

What I believe I have discovered, and it's been said before, is that the war on drugs is thousands of miles long, but it's only about a quarter-inch deep. That's my belief. I do understand my value in all this. I've been given the stage, and I understand that. And I'm trying to make the most out of having been given the stage. I'm trying to communicate what I believe in. I believe in this issue. I believe that drugs are bad, but I believe that we need to stop arresting and locking up the entire country.

PART II

THE CONSTITUTION AND THE DRUG WAR

3. The Illegitimate War on Drugs

Roger Pilon

In America we think it important that government and governmental powers be legitimate. Indeed, every Fourth of July we take great pride in tracing our heritage as a nation to our founding document, the Declaration of Independence. Eleven years after the Founders wrote that document, they wrote another, the Constitution of the United States of America, through which we reconstituted ourselves as a nation. The Constitution continues today as the basic law of the land, the ultimate source of whatever legitimacy government and its powers may have. If a power cannot be traced to the Constitution, or is exercised contrary to protections afforded by it, the power is illegitimate. In essence, legitimacy is just that simple.

Despite the intent of the Founders to institute legitimate government—to derive government's "*just* powers from the consent of the governed" and to limit the scope of that consent by the rights of individuals to life, liberty, and the pursuit of happiness—governments in America today, especially the federal government, exercise vast powers not remotely grounded in or permitted by the Constitution. In no case is that more true, perhaps, than with the massive "war on drugs" the federal government has been waging for more than 20 years now. Our cities have been devastated, our prisons have been filled, our institutions have been corrupted, and our rights have been trampled and lost, all in a futile effort to stop some of us from consuming substances that others of us think should not be consumed, substances that have been consumed by people from time immemorial.

Those consequences of the modern war on drugs will be discussed at length by others in this volume. My purpose here is rather different—and more simple. It is to show the constitutional illegitimacy of the drug war, not the devastation it has produced. More narrowly still, my purpose is to show not that the war is illegitimate because it involves massive violations of our rights—the subject of another chapter in the volume—but because it is conducted without constitutional authority. In brief, I want to ask the drug warriors that most basic of constitutional questions: "Where in the Constitution do you find authority for what you are doing?" Given our Constitution, they will be hard-pressed to answer.

In the course of showing that the drug war is constitutionally illegitimate, I will address several basic questions of moral, political, and legal theory as they manifest themselves in the constitutional doctrine of enumerated powers and the federalism that flows from it. And that will take us in turn to some of the more embarrassing aspects of the drug war as it is waged against the people in their states, several of which have enacted medical marijuana measures in recent years. Indeed, no recent issue has more clearly brought to the surface the hypocrisy that surrounds those drug warriors who profess also to be federalists.

A Constitution of Delegated and Enumerated Powers

We are fortunate in this nation to have a set of founding documents to repair to when questions about legitimacy arise. Although the Constitution is our fundamental law, its often broad language is illuminated by the Declaration of Independence, in which the Founders set forth their philosophy of government—which informed the Constitution in large measure. The purpose of the Declaration, of course, was to declare our "separate and equal Station" and to justify that separation out of "a decent Respect to the Opinions of Mankind." The Founders did that by appealing, in the natural law tradition, to reason, to certain "self-evident" truths: that "all Men are created equal, that they are endowed by their Creator with certain unalienable Rights, that among these are Life, Liberty, and the Pursuit of Happiness." There, in a nutshell, is the moral order. We're all equal, as defined by our rights, which means that no one has rights superior to those of anyone else. We're born with those rights; we don't get them from government. And the rights with which we're born can be reduced to a single idea—freedom. In a free society, each of us is free to pursue happiness as he thinks best, by his own lights, provided only that he respect the equal rights of others to do the same. Thus, the Declaration makes no claim about what may make anyone happy. It implies only that, whatever it may be, we must respect the rights of others to pursue it, as they see fit, while we pursue our own.

Only after setting forth that fundamental moral order did the Founders turn to the question of government, which is instituted, they said, "to secure these rights," its just Powers derived "from the Consent of the Governed." Government is thus twice limited: by its ends, to secure our rights; and by its means, which require our consent if they are to be legitimate.[1]

All power originates, therefore, with the people, who give government whatever powers it has. We see that in the Constitution that was drafted some 11 years later, which begins, "We the people ... do ordain and establish this Constitution." That principle is repeated in the very first sentence of Article I: "All legislative powers herein granted shall be vested in a Congress." By implication, not all powers were "herein granted," as the rest of the document makes clear, especially Article I, section 8. And in the final documentary evidence of the founding period, the Tenth Amendment, the principle is recapitulated, as if for emphasis: "The powers not delegated to the United States by the Constitution, nor prohibited by it to the States, are reserved to the States respectively, or to the people." In sum, the Constitution is a document of delegated, enumerated, and thus limited powers.

That the doctrine of enumerated powers was meant to be our principal protection against overweening government is no better illustrated than by our having gone for two years without a bill of rights—even if the Bill of Rights has come today to be our main defense. Indeed, delegates to the Constitutional Convention resisted proposals to add such a bill by noting that one was unnecessary: "Why declare that things shall not be done which there is no power to do?" asked Alexander Hamilton.[2] When it became clear that a bill of rights would be needed to ensure ratification, a second objection—that enumerating only certain rights would be construed as denying others—was addressed by the Ninth Amendment: "The enumeration in the Constitution of certain rights shall not be construed to deny or disparage others retained by the people."[3] Thus, the Ninth and Tenth Amendments sum up, fittingly, the philosophy of the Declaration. The people have rights, both enumerated and

---

[1] I have discussed the theory of the Declaration more fully in Roger Pilon, "The Purpose and Limits of Government," Cato's Letters, no. 13 (Washington: Cato Institute, 1999).

[2] The Federalist no. 84 (Modern Library edition, 1937), p. 559.

[3] See Randy Barnett, *The Rights Retained by the People* (Fairfax, Va.: George Mason University Press, 1989).

unenumerated. The government's powers, by contrast, are strictly enumerated: if a power has not been delegated by the people and is thus not enumerated in the document, it is reserved to the states or to the people.[4]

Rewriting the Constitution

That conception of limited government, grounded in the doctrine of delegated and enumerated powers, held for the most part until the New Deal, when the Supreme Court, under extraordinary pressure from President Franklin Roosevelt, radically reinterpreted the Constitution. To appreciate the change that took place then—and why it is that someone like White House drug czar Barry McCaffrey can write today, without blushing, that "the Constitution of the United States articulates the obligation of the federal government to uphold the public good"[5]—it is necessary at least to outline that change. For the striking thing about McCaffrey's remark is not its inconsistency with the Constitution as understood today but its very consistency with the modern understanding. Most Americans today do believe that the federal government has vast—indeed, all but unlimited—power to "uphold the public good." Thus, when McCaffrey goes on to say that "drug abuse diminishes the potential of citizens for growth and development,"[6] they believe, with him, that that is sufficient ground for government's having authority to regulate such things. How, then, did we go from a government of enumerated powers to one with powers that are effectively unenumerated?

The answer begins, as most do, in the realm of ideas, which in time shape political events. With the rise of Progressivism toward the end of the 19th century, we started to change our conception of government fundamentally. No longer did we think of it as a "necessary evil," instituted for the limited purpose of securing our rights, as the Founders had thought of government. Instead, government came gradually to be seen as an engine of good, an institution to solve all manner of social and economic problems—through social engineering informed by "progressive" thought. In-

[4]See Roger Pilon, "The Forgotten Ninth and Tenth Amendments," *Cato Policy Report* 13, no. 5 (September/October 1991), p. 1.

[5]Barry R. McCaffrey, *The National Drug Control Strategy: 2000 Annual Report* (Washington: Office of National Drug Control Policy, 2000), p. 2.

[6]Ibid.

deed, the temperance movement, the precursor of the war on drugs, was rooted in just that kind of thinking. It is more than noteworthy, however, that, when the movement reached fruition in the form of national Prohibition, respect for constitutional limits on federal power was still such that it took an amendment to the Constitution to bring federal Prohibition about. No one thought, that is, that the Constitution authorized Congress, by mere statute, to prohibit the manufacture, sale, or transportation of alcoholic beverages. An amendment to the Constitution was required to give Congress that authority. Today, by contrast, we fight the drug war by statute alone.

On a wide range of issues, however, pre–New Deal progressives were regularly testing constitutional limits in the courts, and almost as regularly being rebuffed. As Madison had hoped, the courts were serving, for the most part, as the bulwark of our liberties. With the advent of the Depression, however, the political activism of the progressives expanded, moving from the states, where it had largely been focused, to the federal level. Thus, the new administration of Franklin Roosevelt prevailed on Congress to enact one program after another, only to have the Supreme Court find most to be unconstitutional because beyond the power of Congress to enact. Finally, in 1937, an exasperated Roosevelt threatened to pack the Court with six additional members. Not even Congress would go along with his Court-packing scheme. Nevertheless, the Court got the message, there followed the famous switch in time that saved nine, and the rest is history.

What happened, in brief, is this. Two clauses of the Constitution, the General Welfare and the Commerce Clauses, both of which had been written to be shields against overweening power, were turned by the 1937 Court into swords of power. The General Welfare Clause, as Madison, Jefferson, and others had argued, was meant to limit Congress's spending power—already limited to serving enumerated powers or ends—by restricting it to the *general* welfare, as opposed to the welfare of particular parties or sections.[7] When the

---

[7]As Madison put it: "Money cannot be applied to the *general welfare*, otherwise than by an application of it to some *particular* measure conducive to the general welfare. Whenever, therefore, money has been raised by the general authority, and is to be applied to a particular measure, a question arises whether the particular measure be within the enumerated authorities vested in Congress. If it be, the money requisite for it may be applied to it; if it be not, no such application can be made. James Madison, "Report on Resolutions," in *Writings of James Madison,* vol. 6, ed. Gaillard Hunt (New York: Putnam's Sons, 1906)), p. 357.

New Deal Court was through with it, however, the clause afforded Congress an *independent* power to spend for the general welfare, unrestrained by any enumerated ends. And any restraint afforded by the word "general" was left to Congress to police—an altogether idle restraint, as history has demonstrated.[8] Similarly, the Commerce Clause was meant primarily to enable Congress to ensure the free flow of goods and services among the states in light of protectionist measures that had arisen in the states.[9] By the time the New Deal Court had finished with the clause, however, it afforded Congress the power to regulate anything that "affected" interstate commerce, which of course is everything, in principle.[10] By essentially rewriting those two clauses, therefore, the Court effectively eviscerated the doctrine of enumerated powers—the centerpiece of the Constitution—and the modern welfare state was born. The restraint afforded by enumeration was lost as Congress's modern redistributive and regulatory powers were effectively constitutionalized.

A Federal Program for Every Problem

What followed, of course, was the relentless expansion of federal redistributive and regulatory activities, aimed at addressing one "problem" after another—from retirement security, to health care, to foreign competition, to agricultural prices, to education, and on and on. Indeed, to listen to recent State of the Union Addresses, one imagines no problem too personal or too trivial not to be a fit subject for federal attention. The drug "problem" is a case in point. McCaffrey is right: Drug abuse does "diminish the potential of citizens for growth and development"—even if drug use enhances life for some, at least as they judge the matter. But alcohol and tobacco abuse can be said to diminish life as well—and dietary abuse too, for that matter. Yet what has any of that to do with the Constitution? Life is full of problems. But only a few were made the subject of federal concern, and they are enumerated in the document. Search the Con-

---

[8]*United States v. Butler*, 297 U.S. 1 (1936); *Helvering v. Davis*, 301 U.S. 616 (1937).

[9]"There is much evidence that the main point of [the Commerce Clause] grant . . . was not to empower Congress, but rather to disable the states. . . . The framers wanted commerce among the states to be free of state-originated mercantilist impositions." Donald H. Regan, "The Supreme Court and State Protectionism: Making Sense of the Dormant Commerce Clause," *Michigan Law Review* 84 (1986): 1091.

[10]*NLRB v. Jones & Laughlin Steel Corp.*, 301 U.S. 1 (1937); *Wickard v. Filburn*, 317 U.S. 111 (1942).

stitution as you might, you will not find retirement security, health care, education, or drug abuse included, even implicitly, among those concerns. There simply is no constitutional authority for the government to address those problems.

What that means, plainly, is that most of what the federal government does today is unconstitutional because it is done without constitutional authority. Startling as that conclusion may be to many, a number of legal scholars are at last saying it.[11] And even the Supreme Court is now revisiting, albeit at the margins, the principles it abandoned during the New Deal. Thus, for the first time in nearly 60 years, the Court in 1995 found a statute Congress had passed to be beyond its authority under the Commerce Clause.[12] In his opinion for the Court in the case, Chief Justice William Rehnquist began his argument with a ringing statement: "We start with first principles. The Constitution establishes a government of enumerated powers."[13] Not for years had something like that been said quite so plainly. To be sure, the question before the Court was limited: Does Congress have the power to prohibit the possession of guns near schools, or is that a matter for the states? But since that decision was handed down, several others have followed, including two in the just-concluded 1999 term that held that Congress is without authority under the Commerce Clause to create private causes of action to remedy gender-motivated violence[14] and is without authority as well to prohibit residential arsons.[15] Again, those are small steps in the Court's renewed federalism jurisprudence—so called primarily because it concerns cases in which the states have

---

[11]"The post–New Deal administrative state is unconstitutional, and its validation by the legal system amounts to nothing less than a bloodless constitutional revolution." Gary Lawson, "The Rise and Rise of the Administrative State," *Harvard Law Review* 107 (1994): 1231; "I think that the expansive construction of the [commerce] clause accepted by the New Deal Supreme Court is wrong, and clearly so." Richard A. Epstein, "The Proper Scope of the Commerce Power," *Virginia Law Review* 73 (1987): 1388. In truth, however, it is not only now that we are discovering the unconstitutionality of the New Deal. Thirty years after the event, no less a figure than Rexford G. Tugwell, one of the principal architects of the New Deal, reflected on the point: "To the extent that these [New Deal policies] developed, they were tortured interpretations of a document [i.e., the Constitution] intended to prevent them." "A Center Report: Rewriting the Constitution," *Center Magazine*, March 1968, p. 20.

[12]*United States v. Lopez*, 514 U.S. 549 (1995).

[13]Ibid. at 552.

[14]*United States v. Morrison*, 120 S.Ct. 1740 (2000).

[15]*Jones v. United States*, 120 S.Ct. 1904 (2000).

either concurrent or conflicting jurisdiction. But those cases are raising the fundamental issue of enumerated powers—and making it
clear that Congress does not have power to address any problem it
wishes.

In all candor, however, I doubt that the Court is ready today to
take on the drug war—or Social Security, Medicare, or thousands of
other things that Congress has no authority to be engaged in. Yet in
all of this, the principles are the same. McCaffrey says that the
Constitution "articulates the obligation of the federal government to
uphold the public good." Where is that "articulated"? To be sure,
the Preamble, which is precatory only, sets forth the general purposes of the Constitution, including "to promote the general Welfare." But the broad aspirations contained in the Preamble have
never been thought to serve as specific sources of power—much less
to have rendered enumeration pointless. Indeed, the Constitution
was "sold" to an often skeptical founding generation on the ground
that the powers delegated to the federal government were "few and
defined," as Madison put it in the Federalist no. 45. That was the
whole point of enumeration—to restrain government to a limited
set of ends. If the Founders had wanted to give the federal government boundless power "to uphold the public good," they could
have. They didn't. And they said why, explicitly and repeatedly.

An Unconstitutional War

Whatever authority the various federal drug statutes purport to
have, in fact, comes not from any aspirational language of the Preamble but from the grants of power found in Article I, section 8, of
the Constitution. Yet no federal "obligation"—or power, properly
speaking—"to uphold the public good" is found there, of course.
The closest to that are the grants implicit in the now fertile General
Welfare and Commerce Clauses. But those clauses, again, were
turned upside down by the New Deal Court, as today's Court is
starting to say. Properly read, the General Welfare Clause, as noted
above, restricts spending for enumerated ends; it does not expand
those ends. Absent an independent power to spend for drug control,
therefore, the General Welfare Clause adds nothing to Congress's
power. Indeed, if that were not the proper reading of the General
Welfare Clause, if Congress could spend to further "the general
welfare," loosely understood, there would have been no point in
enumerating Congress's other powers since Congress could do any-

thing it wanted, pursuant to the general welfare, under the Spending Clause.[16] No, the Founders did not carefully enumerate Congress's powers only to have rendered that effort pointless by the inclusion of an independent power to spend for the general welfare. Enumeration was meant to limit government, not to serve as a ruse for unlimited government.

Similarly, the Commerce Clause, through which so much modern drug law has been enacted, was written to enable Congress to regulate, or "make regular," commerce among the states—and, in particular, to enable Congress to override or address the state and foreign protectionism that was frustrating free trade when the clause was written. To be sure, that functional account of the clause has never been nailed down securely by a Court whose jurisprudence on the subject has often seemed rudderless. It is all but a commonplace, however, that that was the principal rationale for the clause—indeed, for the new Constitution—in the first place.[17] It was out of a pressing need to regularize the domestic and foreign commerce of the nation that was breaking down under government measures the Articles of Confederation permitted.

Since the New Deal, however, the Commerce Clause has been used increasingly as a general regulatory power, for purposes far removed from ensuring the free flow of goods and services. In the 1937 case that opened the regulatory floodgates,[18] for example, the Court upheld the National Labor Relations Act, which had been passed in the name of ensuring the free flow of commerce but was addressed not at state measures frustrating that flow but at private actions long permitted under common law principles. Arguably, in fact, the nationalization of private labor relations that followed has actually impeded the free flow of commerce by introducing economic inefficiencies and encouraging labor disruptions that other-

---

[16]"If Congress can determine what constitutes the General Welfare and can appropriate money for its advancement, where is the limitation to carrying into execution whatever can be effected by money? How few objects are there which money cannot accomplish! . . . Can it be conceived that the great and wise men who devised our Constitution . . . should have failed so egregiously . . . as to grant power which rendered restriction upon power practically unavailing?" William Drayton, 4 *Congressional Debates* (1828), pp. 1632–34.

[17]As Justice William Johnson put it in his concurrence in the first great Commerce Clause case, *Gibbons v. Ogden:* "If there was any one object riding over every other in the adoption of the constitution, it was to keep the commercial intercourse among the States free from all invidious and partial restraints." 22 U.S. 1, 231 (1824).

[18]*NLRB v. Jones & Laughlin.*

31

wise would not occur, as evidence from the vast unorganized labor market suggests. And as the Court fashioned its boundless "affects" test, whereby Congress has power to regulate anything that affects interstate commerce, which in principle is everything, it became increasingly clear that Congress was using its commerce power as a virtual police power—the power to secure rights, the basic power of government, which the Constitution reserves to the states. Indeed, while the Court has often said that there is no general federal police power,[19] it has permitted Congress to exercise what for all intents amounts to a general police power. As noted above, the two Commerce Clause cases the Court recently decided—one involving gender-motivated violence, the other involving residential arson—were, for all practical purposes, police power cases involving powers entrusted to the states.

As a gesture of lingering constitutional respect, however, Congress never says, when it enacts such measures, and the Justice Department never says, when it defends them in court, that Congress acted pursuant to its general police power. It is said instead that Congress is regulating "commerce" or an activity "affecting" commerce—when we all know it is regulating gun possession or gender-motivated violence or arson or what have you. Fortunately, the Court is beginning to see through that legerdemain. But is it any different with the drug war? We all know that federal drug laws, for all their Commerce Clause rationales, are not regulating commerce in drugs with an eye toward ensuring its free flow, in light of state interference with that commerce—the very purpose of the commerce power. No, the drug laws are aimed instead at *prohibiting* drug commerce, just as the recently examined statutes were aimed at prohibiting gun possession near schools, gender-motivated violence, and arson. They are all police power measures parading as regulations of commerce. Under the Constitution as originally understood, there is absolutely no authority for them. Accordingly, they are all unconstitutional and hence, in a word, illegitimate.

Constitutional Limits on State Power

But what about the states? The federal government may have no enumerated power with which to wage a war on drugs, but states do have a general police power. The Court's recent revival of the

---

[19]". . . the police power, which the founders denied the National Government and reposed in the States. . . ." *United States v. Morrison*, 120 S.Ct. 1740, 1754 (2000).

doctrine of enumerated powers has limited federal power marginally; but it has also revived state autonomy and integrity, thus breathing new life into the federalist principles articulated in the Tenth Amendment. For as that amendment says, if a power has not been delegated to the federal government or prohibited to the states, it is reserved to the states or to the people. Since the federal government's powers are not plenary, that means that the states or the people retain all powers not enumerated in or prohibited by the Constitution. And the most basic of the states' powers, the police power, is used by states today to wage their own wars on drugs.[20]

Yet states too are limited in what they can do, and not simply by the limits found in the original Constitution. They are limited first by their own constitutions, which vary. And they are limited also by the Civil War Amendments, especially by the Fourteenth Amendment, which were ratified shortly after the Civil War concluded, precisely to limit what states might do to their own citizens. Prior to passage of those amendments, the Bill of Rights was held to apply only against the government created by the Constitution it amended, the federal government.[21] It was to correct that shortcoming—to give Americans a federal appeal against state violations of their rights—that the amendments were ratified.[22]

Thus, while states retained the general police power under both the original and the amended Constitution, the exercise of that power was subject to federal oversight once the Civil War Amendments were added. Section 1 of the Fourteenth Amendment, in particular, provides that no state shall abridge the privileges or immunities of citizens of the United States, deprive any person of life, liberty, or property without due process of law, or deny any person within its jurisdiction the equal protection of the laws. With that,

[20]As John Locke argued, the police power derives from the "Executive Power" that each of us enjoys in the state of nature to secure his rights. When we constitute ourselves and institute government, we yield that power up to the government, in most cases, to exercise on our behalf. It thus becomes the police power, the power to secure rights. John Locke, "Second Treatise of Government," in *Two Treatises of Government*, ed. Peter Laslett (New York: Mentor, 1965), para. 13.

[21]*Barron v. Mayor & City of Baltimore*, 32 U.S. (7 Pet.) 243 (1833).

[22]For a much fuller discussion of the argument that follows, see Kimberly C. Shankman and Roger Pilon, "Reviving the Privileges or Immunities Clause to Redress the Balance among States, Individuals, and the Federal Government," Cato Institute Policy Analysis no. 326, November 23, 1998; reprinted in *Texas Review of Law & Politics* 3 (1998): 1–48.

individuals could bring suits in federal courts against state officials to protect their rights. In addition, section 5 of the amendment gives Congress the power to enforce those provisions by appropriate legislation.

Regrettably, despite the intentions of those who wrote and ratified the Fourteenth Amendment, the history of its use has been checkered, to say the least. In a nutshell, that history began in 1873, five years after the amendment was ratified, when the Supreme Court effectively eviscerated the Privileges or Immunities Clause in the infamous *Slaughterhouse Cases*.[23] Thereafter the Court tried for years to use the Due Process Clause to do what was meant to be done under the far more substantive Privileges or Immunities Clause. As that effort met increasing opposition from progressives during the first part of the 20th century, the Court during the New Deal largely abandoned its "substantive due process" jurisprudence, turning then to the Equal Protection Clause in a futile search for substantive guidance. As nearly everyone agrees, a very uneven body of law has emerged from all of this, and not surprisingly. For the Court has never systematically invoked and applied the well-grounded and ordered theory of rights that is necessary for principled adjudication under the Fourteenth Amendment. That is what the Privileges or Immunities Clause was meant to enable the Court to do.

The debate surrounding passage and ratification of the Fourteenth Amendment afforded just such a theory, for it indicated the intent of Congress and the ratifying conventions to constitutionalize, against the states, the protections guaranteed by the Bill of Rights and the common law and justified by the natural law that stood behind those sources. Indeed, all of that was included in the rich heritage of the phrase "privileges and immunities" and was meant to be secured by the Privileges or Immunities Clause. The clause was the principled anchor and substantive guide that was lost when a bitterly divided Court eviscerated it in the *Slaughterhouse Cases*.

Nevertheless, here too the current Court has begun, very tentatively, to revisit those issues. In a case decided in its 1998 term, for example, the Court explicitly revived the Privileges or Immunities Clause to limit state power, even if its application of the clause may

---

[23]*Butchers' Benevolent Association v. Crescent City Livestock Landing Slaughterhouse*, 83 U.S. (16 Wall) 36 (1873).

not have been entirely appropriate in that case.[24] And in its just-concluded 1999 term, the Court again limited a state when it found unenumerated parental rights under the Due Process Clause, rights that might more appropriately have been found under the Privileges or Immunities Clause.[25] Thus, the Court's federalism jurisprudence is beginning to limit not simply the federal government, under the doctrine of enumerated powers, but states as well, under the federal oversight authority afforded by the Fourteenth Amendment.

Now again, I doubt that the Court is ready or inclined to scrutinize state drug war efforts under the Fourteenth Amendment. Nevertheless, here too the principles are the same. In particular, the police power of the states is limited in a principled way. It is not a power to do anything in the name of securing rights. Rather, it is limited by the rights there are to be secured, which is why it is crucial that courts understand the underlying theory of rights when they adjudicate under the Fourteenth Amendment.

Thus, in the case at hand we confront the claim of some—including the state, acting on behalf of a majority, presumably[26]—to having a right to prevent others from producing, transporting, selling, buying, or using drugs; and a conflicting claim by those others to having a right to do those things, to pursue happiness as they think best, provided only that in doing so they not violate the rights of anyone. Obviously, as with alcohol, that second class of people excludes minors and, for different reasons, acting pilots, drivers, surgeons, oftentimes parents, and anyone else whose drug use, under the circumstances, would compromise the rights of third parties. That will involve some close calls, to be sure, and reasonable people may reasonably disagree about some of them. But it still leaves a substantial number of people in that second class. And it raises the fundamental question: By what right do those in the first class presume to restrict the freedom of those in the second class when the latter are restricting the freedom of no one? If the Declaration's promise of equal rights means anything, it means that we can interfere with others only when rights are threatened or have

---

[24]*Saenz v. Roe*, 526 U.S. 489 (1999). See Roger Pilon, "'Slaughterhouse Cases' Undone?" *National Law Journal*, May 31, 1999, p. A22.

[25]*Troxel et vir. v. Granville*, 120 S.Ct. 2054 (2000).

[26]For a discussion of why majoritarianism will not serve as a justificatory theory, see Roger Pilon, "Individual Rights, Democracy, and Constitutional Order: On the Foundations of Legitimacy," *Cato Journal* 11 (1992/93): 383–84.

been violated. And here, the drug warriors are unable to show any such thing and hence any ground for resort to the police power of the state. Thus, far from being used to secure rights, the police power invoked by state drug warriors is being used to violate rights.

Were it properly applied, then, the Fourteenth Amendment should be available to individuals to keep states from violating their rights regarding drugs. Quite obviously, federalism principles do not operate that way today in the case of drugs. Not only does the federal government not protect citizens from their own state governments but the federal government actively cooperates with those governments in running roughshod over individual rights the Constitution was meant to protect. Bad enough that the federal government violates rights directly through its own anti-drug efforts. It also ignores its obligations under the Fourteenth Amendment to protect citizens from their own state governments—and even aids states in their unconstitutional activities. Thus does the corruption of constitutional principles ensue from the endless war on drugs.

Signs of Hope—and Hypocrisy

Despite that assault by both the federal government and the states, some states are at last beginning to recognize the rights of their citizens in the matter of drugs—or better, are being forced by their citizens, in most cases, to recognize at least a few of those rights. In the past few years, citizens in seven states plus the District of Columbia have passed ballot initiatives legalizing in various ways the prescription and use of marijuana for medicinal purposes.[27] In addition, three states have passed such laws by statute.[28] And a bit further back, between 1976 and 1982, 19 other states enacted medical marijuana laws of various kinds.[29]

At this writing, the legal status of such laws, due to the supremacy of federal law in most cases, is uncertain. After Proposition 215 passed in California in November 1996, the federal government brought suit, in what may turn out to be the leading case testing the

[27]The states are California (1996), Arizona (1996 and 1998), Alaska (1998), Oregon (1998), Washington (1998), Nevada (1998 and 2000), and Maine (1999).

[28]Louisiana (1991), Massachusetts (1996), and Hawaii (2000).

[29]Illinois (1976); New Mexico (1978); Alabama, Iowa, Montana, Texas, Virginia, West Virginia (all in 1979); Georgia, Minnesota, New York, Rhode Island, South Carolina (all in 1980); Connecticut, New Hampshire, New Jersey, Tennessee, Vermont (all in 1981); Wisconsin (1982).

matter,[30] to enjoin various cannabis buyers cooperatives from distributing marijuana. The trial court granted the injunction. But on appeal the U.S. Court of Appeals for the Ninth Circuit remanded the case, ordering that the injunction be modified to "take into account a legally cognizable defense that likely would pertain in the circumstances."[31] It may be some time before that case or one similar to it reaches the Supreme Court, if one does.

In the meantime, the behavior of federal officials in this matter, including elected officials, is not a little noteworthy. Within days of passage of the California and Arizona initiatives in 1996, Drug Czar McCaffrey convened a meeting of some 40 high-level government and private-sector drug warriors to plan a response to the initiatives and to plan, in particular, how to stop their spread. *Salon Magazine* has just published an on-line account of that meeting,[32] drawn from evidence discovered in an ongoing lawsuit brought by a group of California doctors and patient advocacy groups suing to enjoin restrictions imposed by the government following passage of the initiatives.[33] Especially revealing is a comment made by Paul S. Jelling, Robert Wood Johnson Foundation vice president, according to notes of the meeting taken at the time: "The other side would be salivating if they could hear [the] prospect of [the] Feds going against the will of the people."[34]

Indeed they would. But it's not just the will of the people that is at stake. It's also the principles of the nation. In testimony I gave in 1997 on the federalism implications of the medical marijuana initiative movement, before the Crime Subcommittee of the House Committee on the Judiciary, I noted the draconian response that eventually came from the McCaffrey meeting:

> In the February 11, 1997, Federal Register the Office of National Drug Control Policy announced that federal policy would be as follows: (1) physicians who recommend and

[30]*United States v. Oakland Cannabis Buyers Cooperative,* 2000 U.S. App. LEXIS 9963 (9th Cir., May 2000).

[31]*United States v. Oakland Cannabis Buyers Cooperative,* 190 F.3d 1109, 1114 (1999). See Marsha S. Cohen, "Policy Commentary: Breaking the Federal State Impasse over Medical Marijuana: A Proposal," *Hastings Women's Law Journal* 11 (Winter 2000): 59–74.

[32]Daniel Forbes, "Fighting 'Cheech & Chong' Medicine," http://www.salon.com/news/feature/2000/07/27/ondcp/index.html.

[33]*Conant v. McCaffrey,* 172 F.R.D. 681 (N.D. Cal. 1997).

[34]Quoted in Forbes, "Fighting 'Cheech & Chong' Medicine."

prescribe medicinal marijuana to patients in conformity with state law and patients who use such marijuana will be prosecuted; (2) physicians who recommend and prescribe medicinal marijuana to patients in conformity with state law will be excluded from Medicare and Medicaid; and (3) physicians who recommend and prescribe medicinal marijuana to patients in conformity with state law will have their scheduled drug DEA registrations revoked.

The announced federal policy also encourages state and local enforcement officials to arrest and prosecute physicians suspected of prescribing or recommending medicinal marijuana and to arrest and prosecute patients who use such marijuana. And in what can only be described as an act of zealous overkill, especially in light of last week's IRS hearings in the Senate, the policy also encourages the IRS to issue a revenue ruling disallowing any medical deduction for medical marijuana lawfully obtained under state law.

Clearly, this is a blatant effort by the federal government to impose a national policy on the people in the states in question, people who have already elected a contrary policy. Federal officials do not agree with the policy the people have elected; they mean to override it, local rule notwithstanding.[35]

Most striking to me at those hearings was the reaction of conservative legislators long in the forefront of the federalism movement, long among the strongest advocates for reining in Washington's power and returning it to the states and the people. That reaction could be described only as unbridled hostility toward a citizenry so presumptuous as to resist federal drug policy.

And the hypocrisy—let us call it by its proper name—has not ended. On July 12, 2000, for example, I was invited again to testify before the House Judiciary Committee, this time in support of a bill aimed at restricting appropriated funds from being spent by federal officials in efforts to influence state and local legislative processes, ballot measures, initiatives, and referenda—the very thing McCaffrey has been doing on the state medical marijuana front.[36] It seems that in the last election cycle an assistant U.S. attorney in Missouri

[35]Roger Pilon, "The Medical Marijuana Referenda Movement in America: Federalism Implications," Testimony before the Crime Subcommittee, House Committee on the Judiciary, October 1, 1997, http://www.cato.org/testimony/ct-rp100197.html.

[36]See generally Forbes, "Fighting 'Cheech & Chong' Medicine."

had used appropriated funds to engage in grassroots lobbying against a concealed-carry gun initiative then on the Missouri ballot, to the consternation of certain members of Congress, who wanted to put a stop to that kind of officious federal intermeddling in state and local affairs at taxpayer expense. I entirely agreed with the effort to stop such abuse and agreed to testify in support of the measure, provided I could extend my remarks to the identical problem involving state medical marijuana initiatives. That, unfortunately, was not acceptable.

And so the battle continues, not simply for the minds but for the hearts too of the American people. For in the realm of ideas, there simply are no credible arguments left for continuing this endless war on drugs, as the essays in this volume should make clear. From a consideration of both principle and policy, reason reveals that the war is wrong and counterproductive. It is now the visceral response that has to be confronted, the blind, irrational reaction to calls for ending the war that stop thought when thought is most needed, that ignore inconsistency and hypocrisy that is as plain as day. But that is the subject for another day. It is enough for the moment to know that the war on drugs, to its core, is illegitimate.

4. The Drug War and the Constitution

Steven Duke

America's longest war was declared by Richard Nixon more than a quarter century ago. It has been a total failure in its goal of keeping drugs from entering the country. Whether it has significantly contributed to the reduction of drug abuse is debatable. But there is one arena in which victory has been achieved: The U.S. Constitution has surrendered. In every aspect of American life, rights and guarantees of the Constitution that conflict with the war effort have been nullified. The anticonstitutional effects of the drug war have been so relentlessly obvious for so long that a cynic might wonder whether the Constitution is not the true enemy of the drug warriors.

The Fourth Amendment: A Casualty of War

Late at night, in August 1999, armed men shot their way into a Compton, California, home, set off a "flash-bang" grenade, then ran into a bedroom where Mario Paz, a 64-year-old grandfather, and his wife had been sleeping. One of the gunmen shot Paz in the back twice, killing him. They later discovered $10,000 in cash which the couple had withdrawn from the bank that day, fearing Y2K. The gunmen took the cash. The invaders were cops, looking for evidence against a former next-door neighbor, suspected of being a drug dealer. No drugs or other evidence was found.[1]

Such raids are standard procedure in most large cities and, except in the most outrageous cases, they receive the approval of courts. Police can get search warrants on the flimsiest of suspicion—even the word of an anonymous informant.[2] In many cases, though, the police don't even bother to get a warrant, since they are virtually unfettered by the risk of successful suits or other sanctions, particu-

---

[1]See Barbara Whitaker, "A Father Is Fatally Shot by the Police in His Home, and His Family Is Asking Why," *New York Times*, August 28, 1999.

[2]*Illinois v. Gates*, 462 U.S. 313 (1983).

larly if they confine their warrantless invasions to poor members of minority groups.

The Fourth Amendment of the United States Constitution, which guarantees against "unreasonable searches and seizures" and prohibits warrants based on anything but "probable cause," is a casualty of the drug war.[3]

Since the early 1970s, almost all searches and seizures reaching the United States Supreme Court have been approved. The Court has held, for example, that a search on an invalid warrant does not require any remedy so long as the police acted in "good faith."[4] People may be stopped in their cars or in airports, trains, or buses and submitted to questioning and dog sniffs.[5] Police may search an open field without warrant or cause, even if it has "no trespassing" signs and the police trespass constitutes a criminal offense.[6] They may also, as in Orwell's *Nineteen Eighty-Four*,[7] conduct close helicopter surveillance of our homes and backyards.[8] They may also search our garbage cans without cause.[9] If they have "reasonable suspicion," the police may even search our bodies. Mobile homes, closed containers within cars,[10] as well as cars themselves may be searched without a warrant.

The Court has also held that a suspected "balloon swallower" may, without warrant or probable cause, be seized as she arrives from abroad at the airport, strip-searched and ordered to remain incommunicado until she defecates over a wastebasket under the watchful eye of matrons. Validating such an 18-hour ordeal, Chief Justice Rehnquist listed other invasions that the Court had upheld:

> [F]irst class mail may be opened without a warrant on less than probable cause. . . . Automotive travelers may be stopped . . . near the border without individualized suspi-

[3]See Stephen A. Saltzburg, "Another Victim of Illegal Narcotics: The Fourth Amendment, As Illustrated by the Open Fields Doctrine," *University of Pittsburgh Law Review*, 48 (1986): 1.

[4]*United States v. Leon*, 468 U.S. 897 (1984).

[5]See *Florida v. Bostwick*, 111 S. Ct. 2382 (1991); *United States v. Place*, 462 U.S. 696 (1983).

[6]*Oliver v. United States*, 466 U.S. 170 (1984).

[7]George Orwell, *Nineteen Eighty-Four* (New York: Harcourt, Brace & World, 1949), p. 4.

[8]*Florida v. Riley*, 488 U.S. 455 (1989).

[9]*California v. Greenwood*, 486 U.S. 35 (1988).

[10]*California v. Acevedo*, 111 S. Ct. 1982 (1991).

cion even if the stop is based largely on ethnicity ... and
boats on inland waters with ready access to the sea may be
hailed and boarded with no suspicion whatever.[11]

Those incursions, Chief Justice Rehnquist said, are responsive to
"the veritable national crises in law enforcement caused by smuggling of illegal narcotics."[12]

Searches or seizures have been upheld on nothing more than
suspicion that drugs are being transported. Sufficient suspicion can
be mustered by matching the victim of the search with a few of the
characteristics contained in secret "drug courier profiles" that rely
heavily upon ethnic stereotypes. As a result of such profiles, hundreds of innocent people are subjected to indignities every day.

Hispanics bear the major brunt of profiling near the southern
border, but young African-Americans suffer from it wherever they
go. An African-American who drives a car with an out-of-state license plate is likely to be stopped almost anywhere in America. A
survey of car stoppings on the New Jersey turnpike revealed that
although only 4.7% of the cars were driven by blacks with out-of-state plates, 80% of the drug arrests were of such people.[13] The
Pittsburgh Press examined 121 cases in which travelers were
searched and no drugs were found. Seventy-seven percent of the
people were black, Hispanic, or Asian.[14] In Memphis, about 75 percent of airline travelers stopped by drug police in 1989 were black
yet only 4 percent of the flying public is black.[15]

Almost as offensive as relying on racial characteristics in a profile
to justify searches or seizures is permitting the trivial and subjective
profile characteristics to count as "reasonable" or "articulable" suspicion. Federal Circuit Judge Warren Ferguson observed that the
DEA's profiles have a "chameleon-like way of adapting to any particular set of observations."[16] In one case, a suspicious circumstance
(profile characteristic) was deplaning first.[17] In another, it was de-

---

[11]*United States v. Montoya De Hernandez*, 473 U.S. 531, 538 (1985).

[12]Ibid.

[13]Joseph F. Sullivan, "New Jersey Police Are Accused of Minority Arrest Campaigns," *New York Times*, February 19, 1990.

[14]Andrew Schneider and Mary Pat Flaherty, *Presumed Guilty: The Law's Victims in the War on Drugs* (reprinted from the *Pittsburgh Press*, August 11–16, 1991).

[15]Ibid., 12.

[16]*United States v. Sokolow*, 831 F.2d 1413, 1418 (9th Cir. 1987).

[17]*United States v. Moore*, 675 F.2d 802 (6th Cir. 1982).

planing last.[18] In a third, it was deplaning in the middle.[19] A one-way ticket was said to be a suspicious circumstance in one case;[20] a round-trip ticket was suspicious in another.[21] Taking a nonstop flight was suspicious in one case,[22] while changing planes was suspicious in another.[23] Traveling alone fit a profile in one case,[24] having a companion did so in another.[25] Behaving nervously was a tip-off in one case,[26] acting calmly was the tip-off in another.[27]

As even their users admit, the profiles are self-fulfilling. If the profiles are based on who is searched and found guilty, the guilty will necessarily fit the profiles. The DEA claims to catch 3,000 or more drug violators through the profiles,[28] but no records are kept of how many people are hassled, detained, or searched to produce the 3,000. Amazingly, the DEA keeps no records of the *failures* of the profile system.

And what of the cherished right to the privacy of bedroom and telephone conversations? An elaborate federal statute seeks to prohibit most interceptions of such conversations that are not approved by a court order, upon an application establishing probable cause, necessity, and several other requirements.[29] However, the granting of wiretap and eavesdropping applications appears to be even more routine than the rubber-stamping of search warrants. In 1991, 856 requests were submitted to federal judges; *each and every one* of the applications was approved.[30] Sixty-one percent of the surveillances were of suspected drug dealers.[31] In 1998, 72 percent of the applications were for drug suspects.[32]

Not all of the court rulings against Fourth Amendment rights

[18]*United States v. Mendenhall*, 446 U.S. 544, 564 (1980).
[19]*United States v. Buenaventura-Ariza*, 615 F.2d 29, 32 (2d Cir. 1980).
[20]*United States v. Sullivan*, 625 F.2d 9, 12 (4th Cir. 1980).
[21]*United States v. Craemer*, 555 F.2d 594, 595 (6th Cir. 1977).
[22]*United States v. McCaleb*, 552 F.2d 717, 720 (6th Cir. 1977).
[23]*United States v. Sokolow*, 808 F.2d 1366, 1370 (9th Cir. 1987).
[24]*United States v. Smith*, 574 F.2d 882, 883 (6th Cir. 1978).
[25]*United States v. Fry*, 622 F.2d 1218, 1219 (5th Cir. 1980).
[26]*United States v. Andrews*, 600 F.2d 563, 565 (6th Cir. 1979).
[27]*United States v. Himmelwright*, 551 F.2d 991, 992 (5th Cir. 1977).
[28]Tom Morganthau, "Uncivil Liberties," *Newsweek*, April 23, 1990, p. 18.
[29]18 U.S.C. §2516.
[30]"Big Brother Is Napping," *National Law Journal*, May 16, 1992, p. 119.
[31]Ibid.
[32]Administrative Office of United States Courts, *1998 Wiretap Report*, p. 9.

have occurred in drug cases, but most of them have. The drug war fuels the attack on privacy even in cases not directly dealing with drugs. The pressure to uphold police activities in drug cases generates new "principles" that thereafter apply to everyone, whether or not drugs are involved. If the police are authorized to search for drugs on suspicion, they can also search for evidence of tax evasion, gambling, mail fraud, pornography, bribery, and any other offense. The putative object of a police search does not limit what can be confiscated. If police conduct a lawful search, they can take and use any evidence they see, however unrelated it may be to what got them into the home—or the body—in the first place. The Supreme Court has amended the Fourth Amendment's "probable cause" to mean, in most cases, only "suspicion." It has created a dozen or more exceptions to the search warrant requirement. And it has virtually eliminated legal remedies for those few searches that remain illegal. The exclusionary rule—which forbids use of illegally obtained evidence—has been restricted to the point of nullity.[33] The rule does not apply to grand jury proceedings, to civil cases, or to sentencing procedures. It does not apply even in a criminal trial where defendant has the temerity to testify in his own defense, for the illegally obtained evidence can then be used to "impeach" the defendant as a witness.[34] Thus, the police have strong incentives to violate the few meager Fourth Amendment rights that remain intact, because there is in most cases no practical remedy for their violations.

Students and Other Quasi People

Although students in our public schools are "people" protected in theory by the Bill of Rights, they are treated otherwise in practice. The Supreme Court approved the search of a high school student's purse on reasonable "suspicion" that the search will turn up evidence that the student has violated either the law or the rules of the school.[35] Courts uphold searches of lockers and even college dorm rooms on the same flimsy justification.[36] Students

---

[33]Steven Duke, "Making *Leon* Worse," *Yale Law Journal* 95 (1986): 1414.

[34]*United States v. Havens*, 445 U.S. 620 (1980).

[35]*New Jersey v. T.L.O.*, 469 U.S. 325 (1985).

[36]Wayne LaFave & Jerold Israel, *Criminal Procedure*, 2d ed. (St. Paul, Minn.: West Publishing Co., 1992), p. 232.

have been subjected to strip searches,[37] and to having their activities in a bathroom recorded on film.[38] One federal court even upheld the strip search of a male student because his crotch, a teacher thought, was "too well-endowed."[39] The search revealed no contraband. The Supreme Court has upheld mandatory drug testing of student athletes[40] and some lower courts have upheld it for virtually all students.[41] If such testing becomes commonplace it is hard to imagine that it will be confined to drug searches. The substances taken for drug tests will also reveal pregnancy and countless genetic secrets.

If students get only a diluted version of an already watered-down Fourth Amendment, at least they have standing to complain. But aliens who are searched abroad by our drug agents apparently have no rights at all. Upholding the warrantless search of a defendant's home in Mexico by American DEA agents, Chief Justice Rehnquist declared that nonresident aliens are not "people" protected by the Constitution even if, as in the case before the Court, the victim of the search had been taken to the United States and was being held here for trial while the search was conducted in Mexico to help convict him here.[42] Thus, unless they are acting against American citizens or resident aliens, our police can do anything anywhere abroad to anyone. The inalienable rights the Declaration of Independence proclaimed do not apply to foreigners. It is not even clear that American citizens enjoy protection against government actions outside our borders.

In 1992, the Supreme Court upheld the DEA-supervised kidnapping of a criminal suspect in Mexico and his forceful abduction to the United States for trial. Nothing in either the Constitution or the extradition treaty with Mexico, the Court held, required any remedy for the kidnapping.[43] It doesn't matter who the police kidnap, or

[37]*Williams v. Ellington*, 936 F.2d 881 (6th Cir. 1991).

[38]"Camera in School Bathroom Curbs Vandalism but Sets Off Debate," *New York Times*, March 22, 1992.

[39]*Cornfield v. Consolidated High School District 230*, 1992 U.S. Dist. LEXIS 2913 (N.D. Ill. March 12, 1992); Jerry Shnay, "Stripsearch of Student Is Ruled OK by Judge," *Chicago Tribune*, March 22, 1992.

[40]*Vernonia School District v. Acton*, 515 U.S. 646, 115 S.Ct. 2386 (1988).

[41]*Todd v. Rush County Schools*, 133 F.3d 984 (7th Cir. 1998) (students engaging in any extracurricular activity or driving to school).

[42]*United States v. Verdugo-Urquidez*, 494 U.S. 259 (1990).

[43]*United States v. Alvarez-Machain*, 112 S. Ct. 2188 (1992).

where they kidnap them, or how they do it; the kidnapping will not prevent the victim's own criminal trial.

The Attack on Defense Lawyers

What the drug war has done to the Fourth Amendment, it has also done to the Sixth. The Sixth Amendment guarantees, among other things, that in "all criminal prosecutions" the accused shall enjoy "the Assistance of Counsel for his Defense." No other right is as precious to one accused of crime as the right of counsel. A loyal, competent lawyer is essential for the protection of every other right the defendant has, including the right to a fair trial.

In recognition of that fact, the definition of the enemy in the war against drugs has been expanded. Not only are drug sellers and drug users targets, so are their lawyers.[44] Criminal defense lawyers have increasingly come to expect their law offices to be searched, their phones tapped, or their offices bugged. Prosecutors frequently serve subpoenas on defense lawyers prior to trial, requiring them to produce documents and testify about their clients before a grand jury.[45] Having thus driven a wedge between client and attorney, creating a disqualifying conflict of interest at worst and mistrust of the lawyer at least, the prosecutor is then in a strong position to extract a guilty plea. The courts have upheld all these practices, the effect of which is to deprive the accused of his only real defensive armament.[46]

The Supreme Court added a powerful missile to the government's arsenal when it held in 1989 that federal authorities could freeze and later obtain the forfeiture of the assets of a person *accused* of a drug crime, so that he would have no money with which to pay a lawyer.[47]

The centuries-old tradition that confidential conversations between a lawyer and client cannot be divulged without the client's consent also seems headed for the museum of American legal his-

[44]William Genego, "The New Adversary," *Brooklyn Law Review* 54 (1988): 781.

[45]Fred Zacharias, "A Critical Look at Rules Governing Grand Jury Subpoenas of Attorneys," *Minnesota Law Review* 76 (1992): 917.

[46]A federal court has even held that a state ethics rule that requires prosecutors to get court approval before subpoenaing attorneys to snitch on their clients is unenforceable against federal prosecutors. *Baylson v. Disciplinary Board*, 764 F.Supp. 328 (ED. Pa. 1991) aff'd. 975 F.2d 102 (3d Cir. 1992).

[47]*Caplin & Drysdale, Chartered v. United States*, 109 S. Ct. 2646 (1989).

tory. Courts have held that because "monitoring" of conversations in jails and prisons is well-known, any attorney-client conversations that are eavesdropped upon are fair game—they have been implicitly "consented" to. This absurd fiction was even applied to Colonel Manuel Noriega, who barely speaks English. After he was kidnapped in Panama and thrown in a Miami jail, his phone conversations with his lawyers were "monitored." A federal court found he waived his rights by talking to his lawyers on the phone.[48]

Prosecutorial Crimes Go Unpunished

Some prosecutors don't stop at making grand jury witnesses out of criminal defense counsel. They even arm traitorous defense lawyers with bugging devices and direct them to get incriminating admissions directly from their clients' lips. Novelist Scott Turow, when a federal prosecutor in Chicago, did exactly that. An attorney named Marvin Glass came under suspicion in the federal corruption investigation dubbed "operation Greylord." To help himself, he cut a deal with Turow to provide information incriminating his clients. Among others, Glass was representing Ronald Ofshe, who had been arrested on cocaine charges in Florida. Turow equipped Glass with a body bug and directed him to talk with his client Ofshe while agents listened in. Glass continued to represent Ofshe for ten months, all the while secretly helping the government convict him and others. The federal appeals court held that while the prosecutors' behavior was "reprehensible," it did not require any remedy; Ofshe had not been "prejudiced" by the fact that the person passed off to him as his lawyer was really a government informant.[49]

Even more reprehensible was a conspiracy between prosecutors, drug agents, and a Los Angeles defense lawyer named Ron Minkin. After representing drug defendants for 20 years, Minkin became an imposter lawyer, working for the government while pretending to defendants that he was their lawyer. He would suggest to the pros-

---

[48]*United States v. Noriega*, 764 F. Supp. 1480 (SD Fla. 1991). See also, *Cook v. O'Toole*, 1998 U.S. Dist. LEXIS 5846 (D. Mass. 1998); *United States v. Pelullo*, 5 F.Supp. 2d 285 (D. N.J. 1998).

[49]*United States v. Ofshe*, 817 F.2d 1508 (11th Cir. 1987).

ecutors whom they should investigate, and even provide evidence against them. When it arrested the targets selected by Minkin, the government would then encourage the defendants to hire Minkin as their counsel, for which he would collect large fees.[50]

The conduct of the government and the defense lawyers in the Ofshe and Marshank cases is not only outrageous, it is a felonious criminal conspiracy, yet I have never heard of a case like those where *any* proceedings of any kind were brought against the prosecutors.[51] In most cases, nothing whatever is done. The possibility of a dismissal in the rare case that is actually exposed provides little incentive to prosecutors to refrain from such criminal conduct.[52]

Defending a Client Can Be a Crime

Courts have also upheld recent requirements that criminal defense lawyers report to the IRS anyone who pays them $10,000 or more in cash, whether a client or a third party. Attorneys who have refused to make such reports about their clients have been jailed.[53] As of 1986, it is also a felony for anyone, including a lawyer, to accept money or property in excess of $10,000 which was derived from specified unlawful activity.[54] It is no defense to a lawyer or any other recipient that the money or property was received for legitimate goods or services, even essential legal services. Nor is it a defense that the attorney was unaware of the specific criminal activity that produced the money.[55] It is not even a defense to the attorney that he had no actual knowledge that the money or property was illegally derived. "Willful blindness" is a substitute for knowledge, and the lifestyle of the client—fitting stereotypes of how drug dealers comport themselves—may go far toward establishing the attorney's guilty knowledge, or willful blindness. Thus, an attorney who represents a person who is charged with a drug

---

[50]*United States v. Marshank*, 777 F.Supp. 1507 (N.D. Calif. 1991).

[51]See generally, Wendy Kaminer, "Games Prosecutors Play," *The American Prospect* (Sept.–Oct. 1999), p. 20.

[52]For cases where courts did not find use of a defense attorney outrageous, see *United States v. Voigt*, 89 F.3d 1050 (3d Cir. 1996); *United States v. Ford*, 1992 U.S. Dist. LEXIS 9352 (N.D. Ill. 1992).

[53]Richard Fricher, "Doing Time," *American Bar Association Journal*, February 1990, p. 24.

[54]18 U.S.C. §1957.

[55]18 U.S.C. §1957(c).

49

offense who "looks like" a drug dealer is at risk of being indicted also.[56]

It has always been difficult for persons accused of drug crimes to find competent attorneys willing to bear the stigma of being "a drug dealer's lawyer," but now that such attorneys are under prosecutorial attack privately retained drug defense lawyers are on their way to extinction—which is what the Congress and the Supreme Court apparently want.

The Rot Beneath the Surface

Court opinions that eat away at specific constitutional guarantees ought to alarm all who value liberty, but such decisions are at least visible and are subject to intense scrutiny and criticism. Professor Steven Wisotsky calls the result of this erosion "the Emerging 'Drug Exception' to the Bill of Rights."[57] A less visible and therefore more ominous "drug exception" corrodes the rights to a fair trial protected by the Fifth and Fourteenth Amendments' due process clauses. In most drug prosecutions, the trial proceedings are ignored by the press and no opinions are written by the trial judges justifying or explaining their rulings. Those accused of crime must rely on the integrity of appellate judges to scrutinize the record and assure that the trial proceedings were fair and consistent with due process. Yet in many courts criminal convictions and long prison sentences are routinely upheld without even hearing argument of the appeal, and without even the writing of an appellate opinion. In such cases,

---

[56]No attorney seems to have yet been charged under this statute, merely for receiving a tainted fee. But see *United States v. Leiberman*, 1997 U.S. App. LEXIS 1057 (1997). In *United States v. Campbell*, 777 F.Supp. 1259 (W.D.N.C. 1991), the government prosecuted a real estate agent for helping to sell a house to one who later admitted he was a drug dealer. The court indicated that his flashy lifestyle and reputation as a drug dealer, while evidence of the defendant's knowledge or "willful blindness" of the illegal source of the purchase price, were themselves insufficient to prove that she knew that the money was acquired from the sale of drugs. In the hypothetical attorney's case, however, there would be more than a "reputation" as a drug dealer; the client would stand formally accused as such. A mere indictment for a drug transaction has been held for many purposes to constitute "probable cause" to believe the accused is guilty.

[57]Steven Wisotsky, "Crackdown: The Emerging 'Drug Exception' to the Bill of Rights," *Hastings Law Journal* 38 (1987): 889. See also, Paul Finkelman, The Second Casualty of War: Civil Liberties and the War on Drugs, *Southern California Law Review* 66 (1993): 1389. Michael Blanchard and Gabriel Chin, Identifying the Enemy in the War on Drugs, *American University Law Review* 47 (1998): 601.

there is no basis for believing that the appellate judges even bothered to read the briefs or understood the issues, much less dealt with them fairly.[58] The prevailing—although rarely acknowledged—attitude in American courts is that any trial is almost too good for a person accused of a drug crime. That attitude was succinctly displayed in a remark made in 1987 by one of the most liberal Supreme Court Justices. The late Thurgood Marshall, a lifelong defender of the Bill of Rights, told *Life* magazine, "If it's a dope case, I won't even read the petition. I ain't giving no break to no dope dealer. . . ."[59] That statement caught the attention of some in the legal profession, but it produced neither a bark of criticism nor a paragraph of protest. What would have happened if Justice Marshall had said the same thing about petitions from politicians convicted of bribery? Or those of securities dealers convicted of stock fraud? But when Judge Harold Baer ruled in favor of a drug defendant, presidential candidate Bob Dole called for his impeachment and the White House said it would ask for his resignation if he didn't change his ruling. He changed it.[60]

The Forfeiture Frolic

The signers of the Declaration of Independence believed, with John Locke, that the right of property was fundamental and inalienable, an aspect of humanity. They regarded liberty as impossible without property, which was the guardian of every other right.[61] These beliefs are reflected in constitutional text. The Fifth Amendment declares that "no person shall be deprived of life, liberty or property without due process of law; nor shall private property be taken for public use, without just compensation." Under forfeiture statutes enacted since 1970, however, both deprivations occur routinely, with the imprimatur of courts. Under federal statutes, any

[58]Steven Duke, "Civil Procedure," *Brooklyn Law Review*, 45 (1979): 847–850. On various ways that appellate courts and others are trying to curtail appeals, see Marc Arkin, "Rethinking the Constitutional Right to a Criminal Appeal," *UCLA Law Review* 39 (1992): 508–510.

[59]Donna Haupt and John Neary, "Justice Revealed," *Life*, September 1987, p. 105.

[60]See Stephen Bright, "Hanging the Judge; Demagogues, Politicians Chip Away at U.S. Court System," *Arizona Republic*, June 8, 1997; National News, *The Legal Intelligencer*, August 1, 1997.

[61]James W. Ely, *The Guardian of Every Other Right* (New York: Oxford University Press, 1992).

property is subject to forfeiture if it is "used, or intended to be used, in any manner or part, to commit or to facilitate the commission" of a drug crime.[62] No one need be convicted or even accused of a crime for forfeiture to occur. Indeed, in 80 percent or more of drug forfeitures, no one is ever charged with a crime.[63]

Forfeiture is a "civil" matter. Title vests in the government instantly upon the existence of the "use" or the "intention" to use the property in connection with a drug offense.[64] All the government needs to establish its right to seize the property is "probable cause," the same flimsy standard needed to get a search warrant. The government can take a home on no stronger a showing than that it needs to take a look inside. Hearsay or even an anonymous informant can suffice. No legal proceedings are required before personal property may be seized. If the police have "probable cause" concerning a car, a boat, or an airplane, they just grab it.[65] Although property may not be repossessed at the behest of a conditional seller,[66] a driver's license may not be revoked,[67] welfare benefits may not be terminated,[68] and a state employee cannot be fired without a hearing *before* the action is taken,[69] a person can have her motor home confiscated without any proceedings of any kind, if the confiscation is a drug forfeiture.[70] There may be a right to contest the forfeiture after the seizure, but even this right is lost if not promptly asserted. Moreover, the costs of hiring a lawyer and suing to recover the seized property may be prohibitive unless the property seized is of great value.

As construed by the courts, the forfeiture statutes also encourage police to make blatantly unconstitutional seizures. Property may be seized without probable cause—on a naked hunch—and still be retained, and still be forfeited. The reason: courts hold that illegally seized property need not be returned if the police can establish probable cause at the forfeiture proceeding itself.[71] It doesn't matter

---

[62]21 U.S.C. §881(a).

[63]Schneider and Flaherty, *Presumed Guilty*, p. 3.

[64]21 U.S.C. §881(h).

[65]21 U.S.C. §881(b)(4).

[66]*Fuentes v. Shevin*, 407 U.S. 67 (1972).

[67]*Bell v. Burson*, 402 U.S. 535 (1971).

[68]*Goldberg v. Kelly*, 397 U.S. 254 (1970).

[69]*Cleveland Board of Education v. Laudermill*, 470 U.S. 532 (1985).

[70]*Calero-Toledo v. Pearson Yacht Leasing Company*, 416 U.S. 663 (1974).

[71]*United States v. $37,780 In U.S. Currency*, 920 F.2d 159 (2d Cir. 1990).

that there was no cause whatever for the seizure; it doesn't matter that the seizure was illegal, even unconstitutional. If the government can later establish probable cause (through investigation of the seized property itself after the seizure), that is sufficient to uphold a forfeiture.

If the government wants to seize real property without notice, it has to get a court's approval, but that is as easy as getting a search warrant. A seizure warrant is obtained in the same way as a search warrant, and on the same hearsay grounds. A six-story apartment building in New York, containing 41 apartments, was seized on such a warrant, which the appellate court upheld.[72]

No civilized country imposes criminal punishment for mere evil intentions; but the forfeiture statutes—since they are "civil," not "criminal"—are subject to no such limitations. A court recently held that a home was forfeitable because the owner, when he applied for a home equity loan, "intended" to use the proceeds to buy drugs. By the time the loan actually came through, he had used other funds for that purpose, but that didn't matter, the court said, because he had *intended* to use the home to secure a loan, the proceeds of which he *intended* to use for drugs. The home was therefore no longer his.[73]

Any activities within a home that relate to drugs are sufficient for forfeiture of the home. A phone call to or from a source; the possession of chemicals, wrappers, paraphernalia of any kind; the storing or reading of any "how to" books on the cultivation or production of drugs. The operative question is whether any of these activities was "intended" to facilitate a drug offense.[74] If a car is driven to or from a place where drugs are bought or sold and is then parked in a garage attached to a home, the home has then been used to store the car, which facilitated the transaction, and is probably forfeitable along with the car. If the home is located on a 120-acre farm, the entire farm goes as well.[75] If only a few square feet of land in a remote section of a farm are devoted to marijuana plants, the

---

[72]*United States v. 141st Street Corporation by Hersh*, 911 F.2d 870 (2d. Cir. 1990).

[73]*United States v. RD1, Box 1, Thompsontown, Delaware Township, Juniata County, Pennsylvania*, 952 F.2d 53 (3d Cir. 1991).

[74]See David B. Smith, *Prosecution and Defense of Forfeiture Cases* (New York: Matthew Bender, 1992), §4.02.

[75]*United States v. Property At 4492 S. Livonia Road, Livonia, New York*, 889 F.2d 1258 (2d Cir. 1989).

grower loses not only the entire farm, but—if it is on the same land as the farm—his home as well.[76]

It is hard to see any ending point. Once any property qualifies for forfeiture, almost any other property owned or possessed by the same person can fall to forfeiture. Notions about how otherwise "innocent" property can "facilitate" illegal activities are almost limitless. When drug proceeds were deposited in a bank account that contained several hundred thousand dollars in "clean" funds, the entire account was declared forfeit on the theory that the clean funds facilitated the laundering of the tainted funds.[77] Where a drug dealer owned and operated a ranch, his quarter horses—all 27 of them—were forfeited on the theory that as part of a legitimate business, the livestock were part of a "front" for the owner's illegal activities.[78] On this theory, the more "innocent" one's use of property is, the more effective it is as a "front" or "cover" and therefore the more clearly forfeitable.

Entire hotels have been forfeited because one or more rooms of the hotel have been used by guests for drug transactions.[79] Entire apartment houses have been lost because drug activities occurred in *some* apartments.[80]

Dozens of people have lost their homes for growing a few marijuana plants for personal use, including James Burton, a glaucoma sufferer who needed the marijuana to keep from going blind. Burton lost not only his home but his 90-acre Kentucky farm.[81] Thousands of car owners have forfeited their cars because they, or someone else to whom they lent the car, used the car to buy or attempt to buy a small quantity of drugs for personal consumption.[82] Boats and airplanes worth millions of dollars have been forfeited because minute quantities of marijuana were found on board.

[76]*United States v. Tax Lot 1500 Township 38 South, Range 2 East, Section 127, Further Identified as 300 Cone Road, Ashland, Jackson County, Oregon*, 861 F.2d 232 (9th Cir. 1988).

[77]*United States v. All Monies ($477,048.62) in account 90-3217-3*, 754 F.Supp. 1467 (D. Hawaii 1991).

[78]*United States v. Rivera*, 884 F.2d 544 (11th Cir. 1989).

[79]Dave Altimari, "Property Seized in Drug Arrests Boon to Suburbs," *New Haven Register*, May 3, 1992.

[80]*United States v. 141st Street Corporation*.

[81]Schneider and Flaherty, *Presumed Guilty*, p. 9.

[82]Seth Mydans, "Powerful Crimes of Drug War Arousing Concern for Rights," *New York Times*, October 17, 1989.

The sheriff of Volusia County, Florida, routinely stops cars and searches them. If substantial sums of money are found, the money is confiscated, whether or not any drugs are found. The theory is that the money is probably drug related. The sheriff says that in most cases the drivers are so happy that they aren't arrested, they don't even ask for a receipt. Such forfeitures are almost never contested.[83]

There are serious problems with forfeiting cash on the theory it is drug money. Even the fact that there are traces of cocaine on the cash is meaningless. Eighty to ninety percent of *all* cash in America has cocaine on it.[84] Police commonly use trained dogs to sniff in and around cars. The dogs usually react positively to cash, which produces a full search. Often any significant amount of cash found is confiscated, even though there are lots of reasons, other than drug dealing, why people might carry large sums of cash.

The difference between such routine seizures of cash and armed robbery is not apparent. It is unconstitutional, but who cares? Not the courts. It is probably criminal as well, but who will prosecute the confiscators, especially if the prosecutor shares in the proceeds?

Innocent Owners

What about innocent owners whose property is used illegally, without their knowledge or consent? Such owners of conveyances, such as boats and cars, were defenseless before 1988, since the theory of forfeiture is the preposterous fiction that the property, not the owner, is the wrongdoer. On that theory, the Supreme Court said in 1974, the "innocence" of the owner is irrelevant.[85] Such a fiction may have been tolerable as long as forfeitures against innocent owners were rare, but in March, 1988, the Customs Service and the Coast Guard went berserk under a "zero tolerance" program and began enforcing the forfeiture law as it was written. They began seizing boats, cars, and airplanes whenever any detectable amount of any controlled drug was found aboard. Yachts and fishing vessels worth millions were seized merely because a crew member may have possessed a small amount of marijuana. The administration obstinately defended its approach despite expressions of outrage

[83]Stephanie Saul, "High Cost of Breaking the Law," *Newsday*, April 12, 1990, p. 4.
[84]Schneider and Flaherty, *Presumed Guilty*, p. 15.
[85]*Calero-Toledo v. Pearson Yacht Leasing Company*, 416 U.S. 663 (1974).

from congressmen who had enacted the law. The result was an "innocent owner" defense for conveyances (there already was one for real property) included in the otherwise hysterical Anti–Drug Abuse Act of 1988. Now owners of any property seized under civil forfeiture proceedings can defeat forfeiture if they can prove either that the offending use did not occur or that the offending use occurred "without the knowledge or consent of [the] owner." Despite the plain language of the statute, many courts are unwilling to lift a forfeiture unless the owners can prove that the offending activity not only occurred without their knowledge or consent, but also that they did all they "reasonably could be expected to prevent the proscribed use of the property."[86] The owner has been conscripted as a policeman to assure that no improper use is made of the property. In a Milwaukee case, the owner of a 36-unit apartment building plagued by dope dealing evicted 10 tenants suspected of drug use, gave a master key to the police, forwarded tips to the police, and even hired two security firms. The city seized the building anyway.[87]

Property owners who decide that what their lessees do in rented premises, cars, or planes is none of their business as long as they don't damage the property, who conclude that renters as well as owners are entitled to privacy in their day-to-day activities, risk losing their property. Such people might lack "knowledge" of drug activities in the traditional sense, but not be able to prove that they did all they should have to prevent the proscribed use. To protect their property rights, owners may conduct background investigations of their tenants, permitting only those who are above suspicion to use the property. In a nation of 20 million illegal drug users and even more former illegal drug users, hardly anyone is above suspicion of drug use.

The forfeiture provisions are not only horribly unjust, they inflict great damage upon our inner cities. They encourage drug dealers and even drug users to invade the property of strangers rather than conducting their activities on their own premises, thus increasing the hazards of property ownership in poor neighborhoods, where owners can quickly lose everything to forfeiture. Bankers have few incentives to lend money on such property, for the bank itself can lose its security interest if forfeiture occurs.

[86]*United States v. 141st Street Corporation.*
[87]Schneider and Flaherty, *Presumed Guilty*, p. 18.

If the illicit use took place before the mortgage interest was acquired, there may be no interest to convey. If the use occurred after the mortgage was in place, the bank may be accused of not taking all available measures to assure that such use did not occur, and face background investigations of its mortgagors, random inspections, and so forth. There is no way that a bank can effectively regulate the uses to which a mortgaged property is put. Its only sure protection is to avoid lending the money in the first place.

Even more dangerous than the destruction of property values in civil drug forfeiture schemes is the tendency of the forfeiture concept to expand to all other criminal activities. When it is so extended, punishment often becomes drastically disproportionate to the offense and the constitutional safeguards of due process are circumvented. Already, federal forfeiture statutes apply to pornography, gambling, and several other offenses, as well as drugs.[88] Many state forfeiture statutes apply to property used in *any* felony. The forfeiture of cars used in sex offenses has become commonplace.[89] Some cities confiscate the cars of "johns" who cruise neighborhoods looking for prostitutes.[90] Other jurisdictions will seize a car for drunk driving.[91] Where will it end? Why not extend it to income tax evasion and take the homes of the millions—some say as many as 30 million—who cheat on their taxes?[92]

---

[88]21 U.S.C. §§853, 882 (drugs), 18 U.S.C. §§981, 982 (money laundering), 18 U.S.C. §1955 (gambling), 18 U.S.C. §§2253, 2254 (obscenity), 18 U.S.C. §981 (savings and loan offenses), 26 U.S.C. §7302 (tax offenses).

[89]*In re Forfeiture of 1978 Ford Fiesta*, 436 S.2d 373 (Fla. App. 4 Dist. 1983).

[90]George Judson, "Price of Prostitution: Your Car," *New York Times*, December 4, 1992.

[91]See *Grinberg v. Safir*, 1999 N.Y. Misc. LEXIS 259 (N.Y. 1999), but see *Montecalvo v. Columbia County*, 1999 N.Y. Misc. LEXIS 256 (N.Y. 1999).

[92]The statutory basis for forfeiting homes and businesses of tax evaders is already in place. The Internal Revenue Code reads: "It shall be unlawful to have or possess any property intended for use in violating the provisions of the Internal Revenue Service laws . . . or which has been so used, and no property rights shall exist in any such property." 26 U.S.C. §7302. Although use of this provision has mainly been limited to seizures of moonshine and gambling equipment, and sometimes businesses, there is no reason—given the breadth of the drug forfeiture decisions—why it can't be employed to take the homes and offices of tax evaders and even those of their accountants and lawyers. A congressman who failed to pay social security tax on wages of his housekeeper could lose his home. Moreover, unlike drug forfeiture, the tax forfeiture statutes have no innocent-owner defense. *United States v. One Pontiac Coupe*, 298 F.2d 421 (7th Cir. 1962).

A Nation of Snitches

The Supreme Court held in 1927 that it was a violation of due process to try a person, even for a traffic offense, before a judge who had a financial interest in the outcome.[93] In 1962, the United States Court of Appeals for the Fifth Circuit extended that principle to a case depending upon a criminal informant.[94] There, a bootlegger made a deal with treasury agents to help them catch specified bootlegger suspects by buying moonshine from them. The informant was to be paid $200 for each of the suspects he helped catch plus $10 per day and travel expenses. He made the purchases, and the suspects were convicted. Saying that such a contingent fee agreement "might tend to a 'frame up' or to cause an informant to induce otherwise innocent persons to commit" a crime, the court said the "opportunities for abuse are too obvious" and held that no conviction could be based upon the services of an informant who stood to receive a contingent fee.

Times—and the law—have changed. Instead of receiving $10 per day and a bonus of a few hundred dollars, informants now commonly receive a salary, bonuses for information and/or convictions, and up to 25% of all property forfeitures attributable to their "assistance."[95] Some informants have made more than $1,000,000 under such arrangements.[96] Informants in a single case, the Manuel Noriega case, were paid almost $4 million and forgiven hundreds of years of prison time.[97] Altogether, federal and state agencies pay over $100 million to informants every year.[98] Despite the vastly increased motivation informants have to frame others, the 1962 decision invalidating convictions based on contingent fee informers was expressly overruled in 1987.[99] It now doesn't matter that the evidence for a forfeiture was provided by an informant who stood to make hundreds of thousands for a successful seizure. Nor does it matter that a defendant is convicted on the testimony of such an

[93]*Tumey v. Ohio*, 273 U.S. 510 (1927).

[94]*Williamson v. United States*, 311 F.2d 441 (5th Cir. 1962).

[95]Mark Curriden, "Making Crime Pay: What's the Cost of Using Paid Informers?" *American Bar Association Journal*, June 1991, p. 43.

[96]See Cynthia Cotts, "Year of the Rat," *Reason*, May 1992, p. 41.

[97]Mark Curriden, "Snitches Score Big in Noriega Case. Defense May Assail 'Bought' Testimony," *Atlanta Constitution*, February 2, 1992.

[98]Mark Curriden, "Making Crime Pay," p. 44.

[99]*United States v. Cervantes-Pacheco*, 826 F.2d 310 (5th Cir. 1987).

informant, who stands to receive a bonus if the defendant is convicted.[100] The contingent fee crook can plant marijuana in the far corners of a farm, or place some leaf under the seat of a car, in the hold of a ship, or on the floor of a million-dollar jet, "drop a dime" and become rich overnight. He probably won't even have to testify: Even if the forfeiture is contested, it stands unless the owners can prove that they had no knowledge of the drugs. Their protestations of ignorance, even if uncontradicted, need not be—and usually are not—believed.

Informants are not the only ones who directly profit from forfeitures. Police and prosecutors do too. Most of the assets obtained from forfeitures becomes the property of the police and prosecutors responsible for the arrests and convictions. Such funds are supposed to be spent for extra-budgetary needs but personal benefit inevitably accrues. Police and prosecutors are often seen driving fancy sports cars, flying airplanes, and piloting boats obtained by forfeiture. James M. Catterson, the New York Suffolk County District Attorney, for example, drives a BMW obtained by forfeiture, which he spruced up with a new stripe on forfeiture funds.[101] Catterson claims that he is not accountable to anyone for forfeited assets or funds. That what Catterson did was legal, the *New York Times* says, "doesn't make it right." The *Times* also questions "the wisdom of asset forfeiture that gives prosecutors and police a financial interest in the criminals they chase." Giving police and prosecutors discretion over forfeiture money also "insults good government."[102]

If there is a shard of moral justification for forfeiture, it is that an owner, duly forewarned, chooses to use or permit his property to be used illegally and therefore voluntarily "waives" his constitutional rights of property. But such a "waiver" theory can be extended to destroy all rights and any liberty. It is a cancer on the Constitution, and certain to metasticize if not eliminated soon.

---

[100]*United States v. Gonzales*, 927 F.2d 139 (3d Cir. 1991).

[101]John McQuiston, "Asset Seizure Is Questioned in Suffolk," *New York Times*, October 2, 1992.

[102]"The Case of the Prosecutor's BMW," *New York Times*, October 8, 1992.

5. Militarized Law Enforcement: The Drug War's Deadly Fruit

David B. Kopel

Esequiel Hernandez had almost nothing in common with Donald Scott.[1] Hernandez was an 18-year-old Hispanic goatherd in south Texas. Scott was a middle-aged millionaire who lived with his wife on a large estate in southern California. Neither Hernandez nor Scott committed any drug crimes. And both Hernandez and Scott are now dead, murdered as the drug war became more than just a metaphor.

One of the most significant trends of law enforcement in the last 15 to 20 years has been militarization. That militarization is the direct result of the drug war, and it is the direct cause of the deaths of Enrique Hernandez, Donald Scott, and other innocents—and of assaults on the persons and property of many more innocents.

The Constitution and the Posse Comitatus Act

The Founders of the American republic were familiar with the dangers of militarized law enforcement. The British Redcoats had helped cause the American Revolution through their enforcement of the customs laws and other policies of King George. The abuses of the standing army in France and other Continental monarchies were well-known to the Americans. In the 1830s, the Texan war for independence from Mexico was sparked in part by the Mexican government's use of the army to enforce the civil law in Texas.

[1]Some of the material in this chapter is taken from David B. Kopel and Paul H. Blackman, *No More Wacos: What's Wrong with Federal Law Enforcement and How to Fix It* (Buffalo: Prometheus, 1997); and David B. Kopel and Paul H. Blackman, "Can Soldiers Be Peace Officers?" *Akron Law Review* 30 (1997): 619. These documents contain citations for many of the statements for which citations have been omitted (in the interest of brevity) in this chapter. I would like to thank Brannon Denning for his helpful comments.

61

The United States Constitution includes many provisions related to the dangers of law enforcement by the military. Articles I and II specify that the militia (not the army) should be used to suppress insurrections. In *Federalist* 29, Alexander Hamilton promised that even though the new Constitution allowed a standing army, there would never be use of "the military arm in support of the civil magistrate," because a strong militia would render use of the army unnecessary.

The Second Amendment guarantees the right of the people to keep and bear arms so that the nation will not be dependent on a standing army. As James Madison detailed in *Federalist* 46, a well-armed population enjoys the ability to resist a standing army, should the army become a tool of tyranny.

The Third Amendment forbids the quartering of soldiers in the people's houses, except in time of war. Quartering had been a notorious form of "law enforcement" directed against Huguenots in France, and against political dissidents in England during the 17th-century reigns of James I and Charles I.

The Fifth Amendment requirement for grand jury indictment before criminal prosecutions (except for persons in the army, navy, or militia in time of war or public danger) prevents the imposition of martial law (rule by military commanders) on civilians.

In 1878, in response to abuses from the military enforcement of laws against moonshining, and in response to the abuses arising out of military rule of the South during Reconstruction, Congress enacted the Posse Comitatus Act to outlaw the use of federal troops for civilian law enforcement. The law made it a felony to use "any part of the Army . . . to execute the laws" except where expressly authorized by the Constitution or by act of Congress. The Act of 1878, as amended, provides: "Whoever, except in cases and under circumstances expressly authorized by the Constitution or Act of Congress, willfully uses any part of the Army or the Air Force as a posse comitatus or otherwise to execute the laws shall be fined under this title or imprisoned not more than two years, or both" (18 U.S.C. § 1385).

The Latin phrase "posse comitatus" refers to the sheriff's authority to call all able-bodied citizens to his aid. In the old West, when the sheriff "called out the posse," he was invoking his posse comitatus authority. For the military to participate in law enforcement would be for the military to act as posse comitatus.

As one modern court stated, the Posse Comitatus Act "is not an anachronistic relic of an historical period the experience of which is irrelevant to the present. It is not improper to regard it, as it is said to have been regarded in 1878 by the Democrats who sponsored it, as expressing 'the inherited antipathy of the American to the use of troops for civil purposes.' "[2]

In *Laird v. Tatum*, Chief Justice Warren Burger noted the "traditional and strong resistance of Americans to any military intrusion into civilian affairs. That tradition has deep roots in our history and found early expression, for example, in the Third Amendment's explicit prohibition against quartering soldiers in private homes without consent and in the constitutional provisions for civilian control of the military."[3]

As another court put it:

> Civilian rule is basic to our system of government. The use of military forces to seize civilians can expose civilian government to the threat of military rule and the suspension of constitutional liberties. On a lesser scale, military enforcement of the civil law leaves the protection of vital Fourth and Fifth Amendment rights in the hands of persons who are not trained to uphold these rights. It may also chill the exercise of fundamental rights, such as the rights to speak freely and to vote, and create the atmosphere of fear and hostility which exists in territories occupied by enemy forces.[4]

The concerns of the Founders, of the Congress that passed the Posse Comitatus Act, and of modern courts have proven well founded. Use of the military in domestic law enforcement has repeatedly led to disastrous invasions of civil liberty. In 1899, the army was used to break up a miners' strike at Coeur d'Alene, Idaho. Military forces arrested all adult males in the area, imprisoned men for weeks or months without charges, and kept the area under martial law for two years. During and after World War I, the army broke peaceful labor strikes, spied on union organizers and peaceful critics of the war, and responded to race riots by rounding up black "Bolshevik agitators." Historian Jerry M. Cooper observes that the army's efforts "substantially slowed unionization for a decade."[5]

---

[2]*Wrynn v. United States*, 200 F. Supp. 457, 465 (E.D.N.Y. 1961).

[3]408 U.S. 1, 15 (1972).

[4]*Bissonette v. Haig*, 776 F.2d 1384, 1387 (8th Cir. 1985).

[5]Jerry M. Cooper, "Federal Military Intervention in Domestic Disorders," in *The United States Military under the Constitution of the United States, 1789–1989*, ed. Richard H. Kohn (New York: New York University Press, 1991), pp. 135–37.

One of the most egregious abuses of executive power in American history—President Harry Truman's illegal seizure of the steel mills—was carried out by the military, which obeyed an unconstitutional order.[6] As Justice William O. Douglas wrote in the steel seizures case, "[O]ur history and tradition rebel at the thought that the grant of military power carries with it authority over civilian affairs."[7]

During the Vietnam War, military intelligence was again deployed against domestic dissidents. This was exactly the type of harm that the Founders had feared from a standing army. The 1970 killings of student protesters at Kent State University were, of course, carried out by a National Guard unit, the National Guard being a reserve entity created under Congress's War Powers.

As the above examples illustrate, there are several loopholes in the Posse Comitatus Act. Even though the National Guard is overwhelmingly funded by the federal government, a National Guard unit is normally considered to be the National Guard of its state (e.g., "The Ohio National Guard") and becomes part of national armed forces only when it is called into federal service by the President (and then becomes part of "The National Guard of the United States"). Only when in "federal status," and not when in "state status," is the Guard covered by the Posse Comitatus Act. This particular loophole has huge implications for the drug war, as we shall see below.

A variety of laws explicitly authorizes use of the military for certain types of law enforcement, the Posse Comitatus Act notwithstanding.[8] The most notable of these laws is the Insurrection Act,

---

[6]*Youngstown Sheet & Tube Co. v. Sawyer*, 343 U.S. 579 (1952): "Even though 'theater of war' be an expanding concept, we cannot with faithfulness to our constitutional system hold that the Commander in Chief of the Armed Forces has the ultimate power as such to take possession of private property in order to keep labor disputes from stopping production. This is a job for the Nation's lawmakers, not for its military authorities." Ibid., p. 587.

[7]Ibid., p. 632 (Douglas, J., concurring).

[8]None of the Posse Comitatus exceptions involves matters outside the competence of civilian federal, state, and local law enforcement: civil protection of federal parks (16 U.S.C. §§ 23, 78); protection of foreign officials and other foreign guests (18 U.S.C. §§ 112(f), 116); crimes against members of Congress (18 U.S.C. § 351); crimes against the President (18 U.S.C. §§ 1751, 3056); neutrality laws (22 U.S.C. §§ 408, 461–62); threats to federal property (42 U.S.C. § 1885); execution of certain civil rights warrants (42 U.S.C. § 1989); broadly defined "disasters" (42 U.S.C. §§ 4401–84); removing unlawful fences from public lands (43 U.S.C. § 1065); and customs laws (50 U.S.C. § 220). I am not suggesting that the substantive laws in question be repealed. Rather, these laws should be enforced by civilian law enforcement.

which allows the President to use the military to quell insurrections or civil disorder (even though the Constitution specifies that the militia, not the army, should be used for this purpose).[9]

The Posse Comitatus Act by its terms applies only to the army and the air force. The navy and the marines obey the act because of regulations which they have adopted.[10] The Coast Guard, which in peacetime is part of the Department of Transportation (and part of the navy during wartime),[11] does not obey the Posse Comitatus Act, and has in recent years become a heavily armed element of the drug war. The drug war has put the Coast Guard very far from America's coast: in Ecuador, Guatemala, and even on the rivers of landlocked Bolivia. So the Coast Guard uses its peacetime status (and the consequent exemption from Posse Comitatus restrictions) in order to fight a war! This real war (with military boats, artillery, firearms, and shooting) takes place partly within American coastal waters, but also over a thousand miles from America's coast, in the interior of a coastless nation. Likewise, the United States Border Patrol has also been sent to Bolivia.

The Coast Guard loophole has become a navy loophole as well: the navy participates in drug war enforcement, but when it goes into drug war combat (e.g., firing artillery at a ship suspected to be carrying drugs), the navy runs up a Coast Guard flag—under the theory that the flag changes the artillery-firing ship from a navy ship to a Coast Guard ship.[12]

Another loophole was created in 1993 when President Bill Clinton signed Presidential Decision Directive No. 25 (PDD-25) which is said to exempt the army elite attack squad Delta Force from the Posse Comitatus Act. Part of PDD-25 is classified, but sources who have knowledge of the document report that PDD-25 exempts not only Delta Force, but also the entire Joint Special Operations Command (JSOC), which supervises all of the military's special forces (Green Berets, Navy SEALS, etc.). Legally speaking, neither Presi-

---

[9]10 U.S.C. §§ 331–36.

[10]Contrast *United States v. Yunis*, 924 F.2d 1086, 1093 (D.C. Cir. 1991) (interpreting statutory language literally, so that Posse Comitatus Act does not apply to the navy) with 32 Code of Federal Regulations § 213.10(c) (Department of Defense regulation applying Posse Comitatus Act to the navy and Marine Corps, while allowing Secretary of the Navy to make exceptions on a case-by-case basis).

[11]14 U.S.C. § 1.

[12]John P. Coffey, Note, "The Navy's Role in Interdicting Narcotics Traffic: War on Drugs or Ambush on the Constitution," *Georgetown Law Review* 75 (1987): 1947.

dent Clinton nor anyone else can exempt any part of the military from obeying a law duly enacted by Congress. But because PDD-25 is classified, any sort of legal challenge is impossible. As of 1999, White House spokesmen deny that President Clinton has ever signed any waiver regarding Delta Force. (Perhaps if one splits semantic hairs, a "Presidential Decision Directive" is not a "waiver.") But during the Waco siege, the White House press office stated that President Clinton had on his desk, ready for signature, a document to allow military participation at Waco.

Finally, as the labor-busting of the 1890s and the political spying of the 1960s shows, the Posse Comitatus Act is enforced only when a federal prosecutor brings charges. Individuals have no legal authority to seek redress of Posse Comitatus Act violations. If the Department of Justice tacitly approves of military violations of the Posse Comitatus Act, then martial rule is implicitly allowed.

The Drug War Loopholes

The exceptions mentioned above are important, but none is as important, practically speaking, as the largest loophole in the Posse Comitatus Act: the "drug law" exception. In 1981 Congress, at the behest of President Ronald Reagan, created a broad exception to the Posse Comitatus Act, and in 1988 Congress expanded the exception even further, as part of an omnibus drug bill.[13]

The new exceptions allow broad military assistance for the drug war. Soldiers may assist drug law enforcement agencies in surveillance and similar activities, although soldiers are still not supposed to confront civilians directly. Military equipment may be loaned to law enforcement agencies, and the military may train law enforcement agencies. The equipment and training may be for any purpose. If the purpose is drug enforcement, then the equipment and training are free; if not for drug war purposes, the civilian agency must reimburse the military for the training and the equipment.

No Oversight, No Accountability

In 1986, Vice-President George Bush and Attorney General Edwin Meese organized Operation Alliance, to formalize military assis-

---

[13]The loopholes are codified at 10 U.S.C. § 371, et seq.

tance to drug law enforcement. A few years later, the military began creating Joint Task Forces, whose *primary* mission was drug law enforcement. The most famous of these Joint Task Forces, JTF-6, was created in 1989. Based in Fort Bliss, Texas, JTF-6 is responsible for the U.S. borders with Mexico and Canada.

JTF-5 is based on Coast Guard Island, in Alameda, California, and deals with the Pacific and Asia. Combined Joint Task Force 4 (CJTF-4) has its headquarters in Key West, Florida, and deals with Mexico, the Caribbean, and Latin America.

What limits there are on the JTFs' participation in law enforcement are being rapidly eroded. One edition of JTF-6's *Operational Support Planning Guide* enthused, accurately, that "innovative approaches to providing new and more effective support to law enforcement agencies are constantly sought, and legal and policy barriers to the application of military capabilities are gradually being eliminated." Some JTF leaders foresee that not-far-distant day when restrictions against use of the military in domestic law enforcement will be abolished completely.[14] Every year in Congress, there are new proposals to use the military in law enforcement.

Although the JTFs were created solely for the drug war, this limitation is disappearing. Early versions of JTF manuals discussed JTF cooperation with a "DLEA" ("drug law enforcement agency"), meaning that the JTFs would be working with agencies such as the Customs Bureau and the Drug Enforcement Agency, whose job descriptions include enforcement of drug laws.

But now, the word "drug" has been dropped, and the JTF vocabulary simply refers to "LEAs." This change reflects the fact that almost every law enforcement agency, no matter how specialized, can invent some connection to the drug war. For example, the Bureau of Alcohol, Tobacco and Firearms has statutory jurisdiction over alcohol, tobacco, and firearms, as well as explosives and arson. But the BATF procures JTF assistance, under the theory that some of the people against whom BATF enforces weapons control laws are armed drug dealers.

More significant than the semantic change is the fact that the JTFs often pay no attention to their legal constraints. For example, the JTF responsible for the Canadian border area provided "counterdrug"

---

[14]See Jim McGee, "Military Seeks Balance in Delicate Mission," *Washington Post*, Nov. 29, 1996 (detailing the expansion of military involvement in the drug war and the desires of some political leaders to expand the military's role in such missions).

sniper training at Camp Perry, Ohio. Among the trainees were state prison guards; while prison guards perform important jobs, the notion that training prison guards how to kill people at long distances has something to do with "counterdrug" activity is ludicrous.

The military's lawyers are members of the JAG Corps (Judge Advocates General). Like all government lawyers, their duties are to the people, and they are required to ensure that their government clients stay within legal boundaries. But in practice, when JAG lawyers object to particular JTF missions which appear to violate the law, military liaison officers for JAG inform the lawyers that objections are "not career enhancing."

An example of what happens to people who *don't* use drugs as a result of the absence of strong checks on the use of the military in the drug war can be seen in the tragedy at Waco, Texas.

As part of the planning for the Waco raid, the Bureau of Alcohol, Tobacco and Firearms went to Joint Task Force Six, which covers Texas, and asked for training, medical, communications, and other support. The JTF-6 staff explained that they could be involved only if the case were a drug case.[15] If the case was not a drug case, BATF could obtain assistance from other parts of the military; JTF units could be used only for drug enforcement. And while military training and equipment were available from other units, BATF would have to pay for military help, if the Waco raid was not drug-related.

Immediately thereafter, BATF began asserting phony claims that the Waco case was a drug investigation; Branch Davidian prophet David Koresh was supposedly running a methamphetamine laboratory.

BATF knew that its allegations were false. In the mid-1980s, after the death of Branch Davidian prophet Lois Roden, there had been a schism in the Branch Davidians between the followers of George Roden (Lois Roden's son) and the followers of David Koresh (who thought him Lois Roden's proper successor). George Roden took over the Branch Davidian's "Mount Carmel Center" at Waco and drove Koresh's followers away at gunpoint. Roden did in fact set up a meth lab. But in March 1988, when Roden was sent to jail on unrelated charges and Koresh's group took back the Mount Carmel

---

[15]Citations for all of the Waco and Ruby Ridge material discussed in this chapter are in David B. Kopel and Paul H. Blackman, *No More Wacos: What's Wrong with Federal Law Enforcement and How to Fix It* (Buffalo: Prometheus, 1997), and in David B. Kopel and Paul H. Blackman, "Can Soldiers Be Peace Officers?" *Akron Law Review* 30 (1997): 619.

Center, they found the meth lab and promptly reported it to the sheriff. Further, Marc Breault (a disaffected ex-Davidian who was urging BATF to raid the Branch Davidians) was the sole source for BATF's information that there had once been a meth lab at Mount Carmel; Breault also told the BATF that the building in which the meth lab was housed had burned down in the spring of 1990.

It should have been obvious to JTF-6 that the supposed drug connection was a lie. The military prepared a memorandum for BATF on methamphetamine labs, and the precautions essential for dealing with such a lab. However, when the paper was presented to BATF agents, they openly ignored the information in front of the soldiers who prepared it. Further, agents from the civilian Drug Enforcement Agency (DEA) who were assisting BATF also expressed no concerns about how BATF was addressing the risks of a meth lab in its operational planning, which similarly should have indicated to the military that the allegation was a mere pretext.

Had BATF actually been planning to take down a methamphetamine lab, its plans would have been far different. Testimony at the 1995 congressional hearings on Waco indicated the potential dangers of an explosion if a meth lab is not taken down properly. For instance, because a stray bullet could cause a major explosion, a "dynamic entry" (a violent break-in, the BATF's method of "serving" the Waco search warrant) would be an extremely risky, disfavored approach.

In addition, the chemicals involved in methamphetamine production are toxic, capable of injuring lungs, skin, liver, kidneys, and the central nervous system and potentially causing genetic damage. Thus, DEA protocol for seizure of meth labs requires that agents wear special clothing and bring other specialized equipment. BATF not only made no such plans, but made express advance plans to use "flash-bang" grenades—grenades that could set off a massive explosion in a real meth lab. When requesting flash-bangs for use in the raid, BATF omitted mention of any possible presence of a meth lab. Had BATF really thought there were a drug lab at Mount Carmel, BATF should have taken advantage of the DEA offer of assistance by a DEA Clandestine Certified Laboratory Team. But the offer was rejected.

Although it should have been glaringly obvious that BATF's claimed drug connection at Waco was fictive, JTF-6 signed onto the mission of "training a National Level Response Team [BATF strike-force] for Counter Drug operations," in "Support of BATF Take-down of Meth Lab." According to documents received from the U.S. Special Operations Command under Freedom of Information Act requests, the Joint Training operation (JT002-93) was approved due to a request from BATF asking for U.S. and Texas National Guard assistance in serving a federal search warrant "to a dangerous extremist organization believed to be producing methamphetamine." The military assistance at Waco would supposedly be "in direct support of interdiction activities along the southwest border." (Notwithstanding the fact that Waco is approximately 300 miles from the southwest border. Moreover, the alleged drug connection was that the Branch Davidians were manufacturing methamphetamine, not that they were importing it from Mexico.)

As Waco illustrates, the drug enforcement exception to the Posse Comitatus Act has been very effective at undermining the honesty of law enforcement personnel, who are encouraged to allege a drug nexus in many investigations for the purpose of getting, gratis, federal military assistance. Similarly, the U.S. Marshals Service claimed a possible drug problem involved with the Randy Weaver family at Ruby Ridge, Idaho, in order to get military reconnaissance flights over the cabin, which revealed no evidence of drugs. (The overflights did reveal a "hot spot," which was claimed to be a methamphetimine lab; actually, the hot spot came from a doghouse.)

According to an anonymous JTF-6 employee, JTF is often aware that civilian agencies are fabricating a pretext for military involvement, but, "the JTF doesn't even care, because there is little or no oversight involved. There's no independent authority looking over anyone's shoulder."

Fortunately, there are still some in the military (and the rest of the federal government) who understand their duties as public servants—even when the only person looking over their shoulder wants the law to be violated. When the BATF asked for the army to participate directly in the Waco raid (rather than just providing training and equipment), a courageous army lawyer said "no," even though a superior officer called him "a toad in the road" and warned that the refusal would endanger his career. The courageous officer persisted, and thereby prevented the disastrous BATF raid from being even worse.[16]

[16]The events were detailed in the 1995 congressional hearings on Waco, and are discussed in Thomas R. Lujan, "Legal Aspects of Domestic Employment of the Army," *Parameters* (Aug. 1997): 82–97, http://carlisle-www.army.mil/usawc/Parameters/97autumn/lujan.htm.

But one cannot always count on genuine public servants endangering their own futures by standing up for the letter of the law. More typical is a go-along-to-get-along attitude that allowed BATF illegally to procure helicopters from the Texas National Guard. (Texas law allows the use of Texas National Guard helicopters for law enforcement only when there is a drug nexus.)

BATF also made use of the Alabama National Guard for aerial photography. The use was authorized by a "memorandum of agreement" between the adjutant generals of the Texas and Alabama National Guards. Even if the drug nexus had been real, there are a number of problems with employing the Alabama National Guard in Texas. Texas law expressly requires the governor's approval for the entry of a military force that, like the Alabama National Guard, is not part of the U.S. armed forces. But Texas Governor Ann Richards never knew about the use of the Alabama—or the Texas—National Guards until after the raid. Alabama law limits the operation of the Alabama National Guard to the state boundaries of Alabama. Thus, the deployment of the Alabama National Guard in Texas was a flagrant breach of the laws of Alabama and Texas.

In addition, the memorandum of agreement providing for use of the Alabama National Guard in Texas violated the United States Constitution. Agreements between two or more states require congressional consent,[17] and Congress had not consented to the Alabama/Texas "agreement." In other words, the adjutant generals of the National Guards of Alabama and Texas executed a memorandum of agreement that purported to authorize cross-border use of the Alabama National Guard, even though the agreement as implemented was in defiance of the law of Alabama, the law of Texas, and the Constitution of the United States. Since the Alabama governor has no legal authority to command the Alabama National Guard beyond the boundaries of Alabama (Ala. Code § 31-2-7), and since the governor of Texas was not even aware of the Alabama Guard's presence in her state, the Alabama Guard was under the practical command of neither governor, and was thus, in essence, a rogue military force, answerable only to itself. It is precisely such military usurpation of civil authority—the destruction of the rule of civil law—which is the ultimate and real danger posed by use of the military in law enforcement.

---

[17]"No State shall, without the Consent of Congress . . . enter into any Agreement or Compact with another State. . . ." Art. I, § 10, cl. 3.

Shortly after the Waco raid, Governor Richards blasted the BATF for having lied to obtain the Texas helicopters. BATF then claimed that a British surveillance airplane, recently brought onto the Waco scene, had found new thermal evidence of the methamphetamine lab. An anonymous BATF source told a reporter that the new drug allegation "was made up ... out of whole cloth ... a complete fabrication" to avoid further criticism from Governor Richards.

As the creation of the separate JTF organizations illustrates, the lack of accountability is worsened by structural changes in the chain of command, which have the effect of reducing oversight. The military's specialized attack teams are now part of the new Joint Special Operations Command (JSOC), headquartered at MacDill Air Force Base, in Tampa. The JSOC oversees the army's Combat Applications Group (heavily involved in training civilian law enforcement agencies in military techniques for the drug war), the army's Intelligence Support Activity (heavily involved in providing military intelligence to drug enforcement agencies), the navy's SEAL Team 6 (also heavily involved in training, and on occasion in actual drug raids), as well as air force and marine units.

Separated from their parent services (the army, navy, and air force), these special operations personnel are part of an increasingly distinct subculture within the military. It is within these units and their isolated subcultures where unquestioning obedience is most emphasized, where American citizen-soldiers are most likely to think of themselves as soldiers only. And it is these units that are often used against American citizens, as part of the drug war.

Direct Military Intervention

On any given day, more than five thousand troops conduct law enforcement operations within the United States.[18] This figure does not include the much larger number of National Guard troops involved in law enforcement every day.

One form of military activity is reconnaissance conducted by the Joint Task Forces. Aerial surveillance uses forward-looking infrared radar (FLIR—to detect heat sources sometimes associated with drug labs or marijuana grow-lights), side-looking radar (SLAR), photography, and remotely piloted vehicles (RPVs).

---

[18]Charles J. Dunlap, Jr., "Welcome to the Junta: The Erosion of Civilian Control of the U.S. Military," *Wake Forest Law Review* 29 (1994): 359 (citing Center for Defense Information broadcast of April 11, 1993).

On the ground, the surveillance includes sensors, listening posts, ground surveillance radar, and ground patrols. It was one of these ground patrols, conducted by marines, which killed Esequiel Hernandez near his home in Redford, Texas. The patrol spotted Hernandez and his goats, and saw that Hernandez was carrying a rifle (as is lawful in Texas). The Marines said that Hernandez fired two shots from the .22 rifle. They tracked him for twenty minutes, and when he allegedly raised his rifle again, a marine corporal shot him with an M-16 machine gun. A congressional investigation found that the marines who killed Hernandez had inadequate training.[19]

This congressional finding understates a fundamental problem with use of military personnel in law enforcement. As University of Zurich professor Hans Geser points out, police officers are expected to exercise a great deal of individual judgment, and to deal with a wide variety of situations. Soldiers are typically trained for much narrower roles, with less personal judgment, and a greater emphasis on immediate obedience to the command structure. Soldiers are trained to attack rapidly and ruthlessly destroy the enemy. The objective is to kill people. Persons trained for this important mission are trained for just the opposite of civil law enforcement, in which the objective is to capture suspected criminals (not kill them), to minimize the use of force, and to act with a scrupulous regard for the United States Constitution. As Lawrence Korb, an assistant secretary of defense in the Reagan administration, observed, soldiers are trained to "vaporize, not 'Mirandize.' "

When police officers kill someone, there is usually a careful investigation, and the district attorney may bring charges if the killing was illegal. When the local district attorney convened a grand jury in the Hernandez case, Defense Secretary William Cohen urged that the military be given blanket immunity for violations of state criminal laws.

Cohen's demand would have astonished even King George III. On March 5, 1770, an incident of boys throwing snowballs at British soldiers escalated into a riotous confrontation between Redcoats and Yankees; the confrontation turned into the Boston Massacre when British soldiers killed or wounded 11 Americans. After the massacre, neither King George nor any of his ministers claimed that British soldiers should be immune from the laws of the Massachu-

---

[19]U.S. House Judiciary Subcommittee on Immigration and Claims, *Oversight Hearings on the Death of Esequiel Hernandez, Jr.*, November 1998.

setts Colony. To the contrary, the soldiers were put on trial (and acquitted, thanks to the brilliant work of defense attorney John Adams).

For years afterward, on every fifth of March there was a Boston Massacre Oration, in which speakers such as John Hancock warned of the dangers of law enforcement by a standing army. Should the tradition of the March 5 oration be revived—with modern examples added?

Legally, military personnel are not supposed to participate directly in law enforcement. This prohibition is often obeyed, but sometimes it is not, and military personnel (such as the 10th Special Forces Group in Texas in 1993, or the Navy SEALS in Los Angeles in 1989) are reported to have participated in drug raids.

Far larger than the number of U.S. Army personnel involved in the drug war on any given day is the number of National Guardsmen. Although the National Guard was created under the congressional war power, and the guard is part of the military reserve, and the guard receives almost all of its funding and equipment from the U.S. government, the guard operates under the legal fiction that it is not part of the military, and therefore does not have to obey the Posse Comitatus Act.

The guard's militaristic law enforcement can be seen not only in sensational incidents like Waco, but every fall, when Humboldt, Trinity, and Mendocino Counties in California are invaded by army, air force, National Guard, and state and local forces, as part of the Campaign Against Marijuana Planting (CAMP). In a typical year, 100 harassment complaints are logged against airborne and ground activities of CAMP personnel.[20]

In California and in many other states, use of the National Guard for marijuana eradication is typically preceded by a declaration from the governor that marijuana cultivation represents an "emergency" that necessitates the use of the guard. While most persons think of an "emergency" as a spontaneous and unexpected event (such as a flood), the Orwellian military use of "emergency" means "something that the governor thinks is a serious problem, even if the problem has persisted at endemic levels for many years." The truth is another casualty of the war on drugs.

The National Guard also provides direct support for large raids

[20]"Trouble in the Fields: Residents Fed up with Anti-Marijuana Drive," *Law Enforcement News*, October 31, 1994, p. 5.

on homes suspected of containing drugs. Typically, the guard will secure the perimeter, while state or local police will enter the home.

The guard's participation is not limited to raiding homes pursuant to a court-ordered search warrant. In Puerto Rico and other jurisdictions, the National Guard provides a large part of the manpower and the heavy military equipment for police/guard assaults on public housing apartments. Backed by the National Guard, police attack public housing projects and conduct warrantless room-to-room searches, while residents are held at gunpoint.[21] Not even King George III had the temerity to order such raids on people's homes; King George's Redcoats conducted routine blanket searches only of warehouses and other commercial property. But today, in the name of the drug war, Americans allow themselves to be victimized by military abuses much worse than the abuses that sparked the Americans of 1776 to revolution.

Equipment

In 1993, Congress ordered the Department of Defense to sell military surplus to state and local law enforcement for use in counterdrug activities.[22] Through low-cost sales and donations, the U.S. military is transforming the equipment possessed by state and local law enforcement. Some of the new equipment is unobjectionable, such as armored vests and Kevlar helmets. Other equipment—such as military transport trucks—is likely to have only occasional practical use.

But the donation program also provides police agencies with extremely sophisticated surveillance equipment, some of which can be used to spy on people inside their homes. This equipment, such as sophisticated night vision gear and thermal detection devices, is ideally suited for conducting warrantless searches inside homes. And as long as the warrantless surveillance is not used in court (but

[21]For a favorable view of these assaults, see Jerry D. Fitz, "Taking Back the Projects," *Police*, May 1996, pp. 56–61. At the end of the article, the following Editor's Note appears: "*Police* does not necessarily endorse the methods used to enforce the 'Mano Dura' program. We are merely reporting on the logistics of the take-overs." Ibid., p. 61. It is very rare for *Police* to attach editorial disclaimers to its articles.

[22]10 U.S.C. § 381. In addition, the federal government's Advanced Research Projects Agency supervises a Joint Program Steering Group for Operations Other than War/Law Enforcement, which brings Defense Department and Justice Department officials together in order to find civilian law enforcement applications for military technology.

instead is used to develop leads for evidence that can be admitted), the warrantless surveillance is unlikely to be discovered. For many years the Los Angeles Police Department got away with thousands of illegal phone taps by always being careful not to have evidence from the illegal tap itself introduced in court.

The military donation program is also introducing huge numbers of M-16 and M-14 automatic rifles into civilian law enforcement—quite an increase in firepower from the traditional service pistol and back-up shotgun.

The drug war has also led to the proliferation of another type of firearm in law enforcement, the Heckler & Koch MP-5 machine pistols, which are usually bought by law enforcement rather than donated by the military. These weapons are sold almost exclusively to the military and police. The advertising to civilian law enforcement conveys the message that by owning the weapon, the civilian officer will be the equivalent of a member of an élite military strike force, such as the Navy SEALs. The ad copy links civilian law enforcement to military combat, with lines like "From the Gulf War to the Drug War." As one criminologist notes, "The MP5 series is the pride and the staple of police tactical operations units, and it holds a central place in the paramilitary police subculture. Its imposing, futuristic style overshadows its utility as a superior 'urban warfare' weapon."[23]

Functionally, the MP-5 is a fine weapon. But when law enforcement agencies are procuring weapons, they need to consider not only their mechanical characteristics, but also how officers in the field will use them. When a weapon's advertising and styling deliberately blur the line between warfare and law enforcement, it is not unreasonable to expect that some officers—especially when under stress—will start behaving as if they were in the military. That is precisely what happened at Waco when the BATF agents began firing indiscriminately into the building, rather than firing at particular targets.[24] This indiscriminate fire apparently killed British citizen Winston Blake, who was not participating in the gun battle.

It is ironic that many city governments, at the behest of the gun

---

[23]Peter B. Kraska, "Enjoying Militarism: Political/Personal Dilemmas in Studying U.S. Police Paramilitary Units," *Justice Quarterly* 13 (1996): 412.

[24]For example, agent Timothy Gaborie testified that he fired 25 to 30 shots in the direction of the house, without looking where he was shooting. "Lift for Defense in Cultists' Trial," *New York Times*, January 30, 1994.

prohibition lobbies, are suing gun manufacturers for truthful advertising stating that firearms in the responsible hands of law-abiding citizens can provide important protection. At the same time, many American cities are equipping their police departments with machine pistols and other automatic weaponry whose advertising (like Heckler & Koch's) *encourages* irresponsible, military-style use of weapons in a civilian environment.

The drug war is also changing law enforcement transportation. On the ground, the Joint Task Forces convey LEA ("law enforcement agency") personnel in Bradley infantry fighting vehicles. Air transport may employ helicopters such as the MH-60 or CH-47, as well as helicopter gunships. Sometimes the transport equipment is driven or piloted by the military, and sometimes it is loaned to the LEA. In addition, the United States Army Aviation & Troop Command (ATCOM) is selling surplus OH6-A helicopters to state and local governments for use in drug law enforcement. Helicopters are also routinely used by the National Guard in its marijuana eradication program.

The helicopter proliferation has had important unintended consequences. Many "patriot" organizations are comprised of members who have been terrified by the appearance of unmarked black helicopters over nearby rural property. These helicopters (which are actually a very dark green) have played a major role in intensifying fear of the federal government. The helicopters are not from the United Nations, but are part of the National Guard's marijuana eradication program. They are flying over rural property as a result of the Supreme Court decision in *Oliver v. United States*, which allows law enforcement officials to trespass on "open fields" without probable cause or a search warrant—even when the owner has taken all possible steps to exclude trespassers.[25] Thus, many rural areas have been subjected to low-level overflights and landings of dark helicopters carrying men in military uniforms with automatic weapons. Who would not be frightened by the sudden appearance of a helicopter with obscured markings and men with machine guns on private property?

As discussed above, National Guard helicopters were also used in the BATF's raid on Waco, under the pretense that the Branch Davidians were running a methamphetimine lab. At least some of the BATF agents on board the helicopters were carrying MP-5 machine

[25]466 U.S. 170 (1984).

pistols, and significant evidence suggests that the BATF agents in the helicopters strafed the roof of the building. For example, Dr. Bruce Perry examined the Branch Davidian children who left the compound in the weeks following the BATF raid. One child drew a picture of a house beneath a rainbow. Perry asked, "Is there anything else?" and the child then drew bullet holes in the roof. *Newsweek* magazine reprinted the Davidian girl's picture of her home with a dotted roof. "Bullets" the girl explained.

Catherine Matteson, a 72-year-old Branch Davidian woman not accused of any crimes, was interviewed by the *Las Vegas Review-Journal*. She clearly recalled seeing helicopters firing through the roof and walls of the residence, stating "I saw the yellow flashes." When machine guns fire, there is a yellow flash of muzzle blast, visible even in daylight. Attorney Jack Zimmermann, who went into the Branch Davidian house during the siege, in order to try to convince the Branch Davidians to surrender, later testified that he saw many bullet holes in the ceilings with a downward trajectory, indicating that the helicopters had been firing into the compound from above. (The holes in the roof flared downward, and therefore could not have been created by people shooting up through the roof into the sky.) There is no nearby high ground from which BATF agents not in helicopters could have shot bullets into the building with a steep downward trajectory.

As former BATF director Stephen Higgins acknowledged, anyone who strafed the building from a helicopter ought to be charged with attempted murder; even if BATF agents on the ground had the legal right to shoot at particular targets who were shooting at them, there could be no legal justification for shooting through the roof into a building known to contain women and children.[26]

Military helicopters with military pilots carried men firing military machine pistols into a building full of women and children. None of the people in that building used drugs. But like Esequiel Hernandez, they too were attacked by the military in the name of the drug war.

Paramilitary Training

The Joint Task Forces provide federal, state, and local law enforcement with extensive training. Among the subjects taught are patrolling, helicopter attacks, sniping, intelligence, and combat tech-

---

[26]Higgins maintains that no one in the helicopters fired a shot.

niques. The combat techniques often fall under what is called "advanced military operations on urbanized terrain" (AMOUT). This is a euphemism for close quarters combat (CQC)—house-to-house urban killing, as practiced in places such as Stalingrad in 1943. Before 1993, official Army policy forbade teaching close quarters combat to civilian law-enforcement, but that restriction has been abandoned. Much of the military training is provided by Army Rangers or Navy SEALs élite attack teams.

Before the JTFs were created, law enforcement agencies still trained their employees. The difference today is that much of training is free (provided with federal funds ostensibly as part of the drug war), and much of the training is provided by military personnel, rather than by civilians such as retired law enforcement officers.

The federal government actively works to militarize local law enforcement. For example, Mark Lonsdale, the director of the federal government's Special Tactical Training Unit wrote that there are various governmental programs, including those run by the federal Drug Enforcement Agency "available to local law enforcement" for marijuana control. "The thrust of this training is towards developing more of a military approach to tactics along with the study of the methodology of the growers."[27]

The United States military has also begun conducting joint warfare exercises with state and local law enforcement. For example, one morning the residents of Cass Corridor (a poor neighborhood in Detroit) were startled by the sounds of explosives and massive gunfire. While many residents hid, the few who dared to look outside found an 80-person Detroit police department practice assault in progress on a vacant four-story building in the neighborhood. The deputy police chief in charge of the practice assault explained that such drills are routinely performed by police agencies in conjunction with the U.S. Army and other federal agencies.

In June 1995, the Chicago suburb of Des Plaines was the sight of another gunfire, explosives, and helicopter extravaganza. According to the *Chicago Sun Times*, when concerned residents called the local police, the police "said they never heard of it." Eventually, the Illinois State Patrol acknowledged that the war exercises were "some sort of SWAT thing; multijurisdictional. We can't talk about

[27]Mark V. Lonsdale, *Raids: A Tactical Guide to High Risk Warrant Service* (Los Angeles: S.T.T.U., Training Division, 1991), p. 194.

it." The Pentagon called the incidents "routine training" for "military police."

One night later, the Chicago suburb of Lemont underwent a similar invasion. The official explanation was "a navigational exercise"—as if shooting guns and setting off explosives were part of "navigation."

In June 1996, 200 soldiers from Fort Bragg conducted urban warfare exercises in Pittsburgh and McKeesport, Pennsylvania, in conjunction with the Pittsburgh and Allegheny County SWAT teams. These domestic warfare drills, with combined military/SWAT/ local police training, are increasingly common, and are another source of "black helicopter" rumors.

The absence of civilian oversight is especially acute in military training for law enforcement. We know that at the infamous School of the Americas (where many Latin American military officers involved in human rights violations and murder have received U.S. training), the number of drug courses rose from zero in 1989 to 90 in 1997. But the training that takes place in foreign countries is legally hidden from civilian monitoring. As a first step to reform, the U.S. military should be required to produce an annual unified report to Congress on all training of Latin American forces, to enhance congressional oversight.

Not only is training of the Latin American military hidden from the American people, so is the training of the American military. Amazingly, all military special operations training (Delta Force, Green Berets, Navy SEALS, etc.) is shielded from congressional oversight.[28]

State and local militarization

A survey by criminologist Peter Kraska reports that 89 percent of police departments have paramilitary SWAT units, and 46 percent have received training from military personnel on active duty.[29] Even if Kraska's figure is too high (because police departments without paramilitary units did not answer his survey), it is clear the local law enforcement paramilitarism is far more common than it was a decade or two ago.

[28]John Rudy and Ivan Eland, "Special Operations Military Training Abroad and Its Dangers," Cato Institute Foreign Policy Briefing Paper no. 53, June 22, 1999.

[29]Peter B. Kraska and Victor E. Kappeler, "Militarizing American Police: The Rise and Normalization of Paramilitary Units," *Social Problems* 44 (1997).

These paramilitary units are only rarely used for hostage rescue or antiterrorism (since hostage-taking and terrorism fortunately are rare). Instead, the primary use of these units is to serve "dynamic entry" search warrants in drug cases.[30]

Serving a search warrant by violently breaking into a house (as opposed to knocking first and demanding entry) is justifiable in certain situations, such as when the occupants are known to be armed and dangerous. But once paramilitary units are in place, they have a tendency to want to keep busy even when there is no need for their special violent skills. Former New York City Police Commissioner William Bratton explained: "In those instances where the suspect might be armed, we would call in a special tactics unit. Over time, though, it became common to use the tactical unit no matter what or who the warrant was for. They used stun grenades each time and looked at it as practice."[31]

The victims of these raids are not just people who break the drug laws. For example, the Reverend Acelyne Williams was a substance abuse counselor in a poor neighborhood in Boston. One evening Williams was visited in his apartment by a substance abuser who also happened to be an undercover informant in the pay of the Boston police. Later, the informant, obviously drunk, gave the police the address of a drug dealer, except the informant mistakenly gave the police the address of the Reverend Williams. The police promptly obtained a search warrant, based only on the drunk's statement. If the police had attempted corroboration, they would have found that the apartment in question belonged to a 70-year-old retired Methodist minister, and there were no signs of drug activity at the apartment.

Armed with the search warrant, and plenty of firearms, the Boston police executed a dynamic entry, breaking into Williams's apartment, chasing him into his bedroom, shoving him to the floor and handcuffing him while pointing guns at his head. He promptly died of a heart attack.[32]

The litany of these victims grows ever larger. In Houston in the summer of 1998, six police officers broke into the home of Pedro

[30]Kraska and Kappeler; Timothy Egan, "Soldiers of the Drug War Remain on Duty," *New York Times*, March 1, 1999.

[31]Raymond Dussault, "The Taking of New York," *Government Technology*, August 1999, p. 66.

[32]*New York Times*, March 28, 1994.

Oregon Navarro and shot him dead. The pattern was the same as in many other drug war deaths: The police broke into his home at night, with no warning. When the victim grabbed his gun to protect himself from the invaders, he was shot 12 times. Navarro had nothing to do with drugs; the search warrant had been based only on the word of a drunk who, arrested for public inebriation, was given a chance to give the police the address of a "drug dealer," in exchange for being released.[33]

While some drug war deaths, such as the Williams and Navarro murders, make national wire services, most do not. More typical are cases such as one that received no national press, other than a brief mention in the *National Review*:

> On the night of April 17 [1995], sheriff's deputies raided the trailer home of Scott W. Bryant in Beaver Dam, Wisconsin, to execute a search warrant as part of a drug investigation. Moments after the deputies burst into the trailer, one of them fired a shot that fatally wounded Bryant. The 29-year-old man, who was unarmed and offered no resistance, died in front of his 7-year-old son. The police found three grams of marijuana in the trailer.[34]

Bryant was shot by a detective who had repeatedly made headline-grabbing drug busts. Although the district attorney found the shooting "not in any way justified," no criminal charges were filed, and the detective was returned to active duty.

The Los Angeles Police Department has been a leader in militarization and aggression among major urban police departments. Future chief Daryl Gates created the first special weapons and tactics (SWAT) team in the 1960s. (Gates had originally wanted to call it a "special weapons attack team," but changed the name for public relations purposes.) Violent break-ins of homes under the pretext of drug law enforcement became routine in the 1980s. In 1989, for example, LAPD officers, including the Gang Task Force, broke into and destroyed four apartments on Dalton Avenue; the apartments were suspected as crack dens but in fact were not. This did not stop LAPD officers from spray painting on an apartment wall, "Gang

[33]Timothy Lynch, "'Drug War' Is Slowly Diluting Constitutional Safeguards," *San Francisco Journal*, December 2, 1998.

[34]*National Review*, June 12, 1995, p. 14.

Task Force Rules."[35] The officers who participated in the raid were promoted.[36] To many people of color in major cities, the distinction between the bad elements in a police gang task force and a non-governmental gang is increasingly blurry. Both are likely to perpetrate criminal assaults against persons and property, based on weak pretexts, and both are unlikely to be punished for their offenses.

As a result of both federal and local actions, America is moving toward the normalization of paramilitary forces in law enforcement. For example, the police in Fresno, California, have taken the next step toward militarization of local law enforcement. The Fresno SWAT team, in full battle gear, now deploys a full-time patrol unit in the city. Deeming the SWAT patrol an "unqualified success," the Fresno police department "is encouraging other police agencies to follow suit."

About 20 percent of police departments in cities over 50,000 have already put their own paramilitary units into street police work. In many cases, funding for street deployment of paramilitary units is funded by "community policing" grants from the federal government!

SWAT teams also get deployed in missions very foreign to ordinary police work. The SWAT team in Chapel Hill, North Carolina, conducted a large-scale crack raid on an entire block in a predominantly black neighborhood. The raid, termed "Operation Redi-Rock," resulted in the detention and search of up to 100 people, all of whom were black. (Whites were allowed to leave the area.) No one was ever prosecuted for a crime.[37]

Drug war violence is often inspired by forfeiture laws, which allow the police to seize property without permission from a court, and to keep the property even if the property owner is acquitted of criminal charges—or if criminal charges are never filed.[38]

On October 12, 1992, a multitude of federal and state agencies (including the National Park Service, the Forest Service, the Drug Enforcement Administration, and the National Guard) broke into

[35]Paul Chevigny, *Edge of the Knife: Police Violence in the Americas* (New York: The New Press, 1995), p. 45.

[36]Chevigny, p. 51.

[37]*Barnett v. Karpinos*, 460 S.E.2d 208, 209–10 (1995).

[38]See Henry Hyde, *Forfeiting Our Property Rights* (Washington: Cato Institute, 1995); Leonard Levy, *A License to Steal: The Forfeiture of Property* (Chapel Hill, N.C.: Univ. of N.C. Pr., 1995); Terrance G. Reed, *American Forfeiture Law: Property Owners Meet the Prosecutor*, Cato Institute Policy Analysis no. 179, September 29, 1992.

the home of southern California millionaire Donald Scott. The no-knock, late night raid was supposedly designed to serve a warrant to look for marijuana plants growing on Scott's estate, although there was no realistic possibility that Scott could have destroyed the marijuana plants (alleged to be hidden among trees far from his home) during the time it would have taken the police to knock at his door and demand entry. When Scott, awakened by the noise of people breaking into his home at night, attempted to protect his wife from the break-in by running into the living room with his legally owned .38 revolver, he was shot dead. The search yielded no evidence of drugs or illegal activity.

An investigation by Ventura County, California, District Attorney Michael Bradbury found that the basis of the warrant—a drug agent's claim that while in a surveillance plane 1,000 feet above the ground, the agent could see individual marijuana plants concealed in leafy trees—was fabricated. The district attorney also noted that the sheriff's department that participated in the raid had conducted an appraisal of the five-million-dollar Scott ranch before the raid, apparently with the expectation that the ranch would be forfeited to the government.

Most forfeitures do not involve violence or death. When law enforcement officers point their guns at someone and announce they are taking away the property, most property owners do not resist. Similarly, in most robberies perpetrated by individual criminals with guns, the victim does not resist and no one gets hurt.

In practice, forfeiture has increasingly become a form of legalized robbery. When the property of an innocent person is taken away at gunpoint, the effect on the victim is the same, whether the perpetrator was an individual criminal with a handgun, or several federal agents with machine guns. For example, two Kansas City police drug squad members, wearing ski masks to conceal their identity, handed forfeiture papers to the owner of a Corvette car, and then drove the vehicle away. The man was not charged with any crimes. Except for getting a receipt, the man experienced the functional equivalent of a carjacking.

Causes of Law Enforcement Militarization and Violence

The collapse of the Soviet Union has, unfortunately, led many military officials to seek out a new enemy to justify continued funding. Often, that new military enemy turns out to be American citizens. The North American Aerospace Defense Command (NORAD) admits that it is no longer capable of protecting Americans from incoming nuclear missiles. Yet NORAD enjoys hundreds of millions of dollars in annual funding, as part of a 1.8 billion dollar systems upgrade, having convinced Congress to assign NORAD the mission of tracking planes and ships that might be carrying drugs.[39]

Many other federal military programs have hitched themselves to the antidrug bandwagon. For example, when President Clinton in April 1996 requested 250 million dollars in extra funding for antidrug programs, over half that money was earmarked for the military.[40]

The incentives for lawless violence and militarization do not come entirely from law enforcement itself. As sociologist Phillip Jenkins observes, "Media images can also frame the expectation and behavior of individual agents and administrators."[41] Sensationalistic movies like *Lethal Weapon* glorify militaristic, violent police conduct in the name of the drug war. While the effects of violent television on children have received a great deal of attention, the effects of violent entertainment on adults, including adults in law enforcement, have rarely been analyzed.

Another cause of militarization is the use of military rhetoric by politicians. Political talk about a "war on drugs" or a "war on crime" confuses the objectives and methods of war (destroying a foreign military force, with no worry about proper procedure) with law enforcement in a free society, involving suspects who are American citizens entitled to the full protection of the Bill of Rights. As New York University law professor Paul Chevigny explains:

> Armies are organized and trained for killing an enemy, usu-
> ally more or less well-defined, and not for service and law-
> enforcement among a civilian population to which they
> themselves belong, in situations for which they have to
> make fine-grained legal and social distinctions about what

---

[39]Jim Malloy, "These Days, NORAD Key Player in Drug War," *Denver Post*, April 23, 1996.

[40]Specifically: $98 million to modify two navy P-3B aircraft into "specialized radar warning aircraft" that would be transferred to the U.S. Customs Service; $15 million to install a TPS-70 ground-based radar system in an unspecified foreign country; $6 million for "non-intrusive" inspection systems along the Mexican border; $3 million more for National Guard marijuana eradication; and $10 million for "classified" Department of Defense drug activities.

[41]Phillip Jenkins, *Using Murder: The Social Construction of Serial Homicide* (1994), p. 233.

> action is required....[T]he results of ["war on crime" rhetoric]
> distort and poison police relations with citizens. The police
> think of themselves as an occupying army, and the public
> comes to think the same. The police lose the connection with
> the public which is a principal advantage to local policing,
> and their job becomes progressively more difficult, while
> they become more unpopular.[42]

One can be in favor of drugs being illegal and still oppose "the
war on drugs," just as one can want food stamp fraud to be illegal
without wanting a "war on welfare cheaters," because to have a
"war" is to make it likely that the military will become involved. As
police studies professor Peter B. Kraska writes:

> [T]he militaristic nature of the discourse on crime and drug
> control—wars on crime and wars on drugs—constitutes
> more than ineffectual media/political rhetoric. Filtering so-
> lutions to the complex social problems of crime and sub-
> stance abuse through the "war" metaphor helps to structure
> our values in use, our theories, and most important, our
> actions. . . . A metaphor and associated discourse material-
> ized, for example, into urban police departments deploying
> paramilitary police groups to patrol U.S. neighborhoods.[43]

Regarding the First World War, historian Randolph Bourne observed that "war is the health of the state." War may not be good for
children and other living things (according to a popular 1960s
poster), but war is wonderful for expanding state power. The drug
war has been the health of the military state, and may in the long
run be the death of the Constitution.

Reform

Congress should make the following reforms to address the problem of law enforcement militarization:

- Tighten the Posse Comitatus Act so that it proscribes all use of
  military personnel and equipment, not just use of the army and
  air force.

[42]Chevigny, p. 124.

[43]Kraska, p. 420. Of course the United States had a "war on poverty" in the 1960s
without sending in the army. But the "war on poverty" rhetoric, along with President
Carter's assertion that energy crisis was "the moral equivalent of war," helped pave
the way for "war on crime" and "war on drugs" rhetoric, rhetoric that has led to real
military intervention.

- Eliminate the loophole that exempts the National Guard from the act when the guard is in "state status."
- Repeal the drug exceptions and other exceptions to the Posse Comitatus Act. Retain exceptions only for law enforcement in international waters or requiring unique military expertise related to nuclear weapons. (The FBI has received massive funding in recent years to deal with chemical or biological weapons.)
- Make knowing violation of the Posse Comitatus Act into a predicate felony for felony murder, so that murder prosecutions may be brought if a death results from deliberate Posse Comitatus Act violations.
- Bar the use in federal courts of any evidence obtained in violation of the Posse Comitatus Act.
- Create a civil cause of action for persons injured by Posse Comitatus Act violations—so that the Department of Justice is not able to nullify the Posse Comitatus Act by failing to enforce it.

In addition, Congress should repeal 10 U.S.C. § 371 et seq., which force the Department of Defense to give or sell military equipment to law enforcement agencies.

Of course, any person who has served honorably in the military should be allowed to apply for any civilian job, including law enforcement. But the federal government should stop subsidizing police departments for hiring persons with a military background, as opposed to a civilian background. Much of the training which makes a good soldier is contradictory to the training necessary to be a peace officer.

In the years before the Posse Comitatus Act, any soldier who did engage in police activity was deemed to be acting as a private citizen, rather than as a soldier. Under this "Mansfield Doctrine," the individual, since he was not acting as a soldier, could be personally sued or criminally prosecuted for any wrongs he committed. Courts should revive the Mansfield Doctrine at once, and allow injured victims to bring lawsuits against individual "law enforcement" soldiers who perpetrate civil torts.

Law enforcement use of masks in the service of search or arrest warrants should be prohibited, except when specifically authorized by a court when issuing the warrant, based on compelling need. Masks not only make peace officers look inappropriately terrifying, they prevent identification of rogue officers so that they cannot be sued later for criminal acts.

As an important symbolic step, law enforcement should give up its black or near-black uniforms and replace them with a color (such as ordinary blue) more consistent with law enforcement in a democracy. Michael Solomon, a Rutgers University professor who studies the psychology of clothing, explains that black law enforcement uniforms tap "into associations between the color black and authority, invincibility, the power to violate laws with impunity."[44]

Conclusion

The militarization of law enforcement has created the equivalent of a standing army engaged against the American people—precisely what was feared by the Framers. The consequences have been just what the Framers expected from a standing army involved in domestic law enforcement (especially enforcement of laws against the possession of certain commodities): the erosion of the Bill of Rights, particularly the Fourth Amendment's protection against unreasonable searches, and the deaths of innocent people.

Soldiers are not peace officers. At all levels of policing, it is time that police officers be restored to their honored status as peace officers. Police ethicist John Kleinig notes: "Were police to see themselves primarily as social peace-keepers, they would be less inclined to 'overkill' in their dealings with both ordinary citizens and those whose disruptive activities properly require their intervention."[45] Cicero's advice to the Roman republic, "Let the soldier give way to the civilian,"[46] must be heeded by those who are intent on preserving the American republic—and the rule of civil law.

---

[44]William F. Powers, "Dressed to Kill?" *Washington Post*, May 4, 1995.

[45]John Kleinig, *The Ethics of Policing* (Port Chester, N.Y.: Cambridge University Press, 1996), p. 102.

[46]"Cedant arma togae." Marcus Tullius Cicero, *Orationes Philippicae* (ca. 60 B.C.).

PART III

THE FAILURE OF DRUG PROHIBITION:
LAW ENFORCEMENT PERSPECTIVES

6. Fight Back: A Solution between Prohibition and Legalization

Michael Levine

The effort expended by the bureaucracy in defending any error is in direct proportion to the size of the error.

—John Nies

The 30-year, trillion dollar war on drugs, despite overwhelming evidence of its failure—from treatment on demand and interdiction programs to its street law enforcement and billion dollar ad campaigns—still grinds onward with ever bigger budgets, wreaking ever more havoc on our Constitution and filling our jails with more people than populate some entire countries.[1] To say the least, it's time to try something new. If my 35-year career as an international federal narcotic officer, trial consultant, and expert witness has produced lasting positive results, they are found in a program that I developed called the Fight Back: Community-Police Antidrug Partnership.

Someone once said that all new ideas begin as heresy. However, *Fight Back*, when first presented in a book published in 1991, was well received. The plan was reviewed by the Swedish Carnegie Institute as "the only drug plan ever to come out of America that made any sense." In 1993 the Clinton drug policy office recommended it as reading for communities with drug problems. It showed good promise of solving much of our nation's drug problem, sharply reducing police corruption and brutality, and greatly increasing police-community harmony. So why, in eight years, has such a promising program never been given even a trial run?

Understanding the Fight Back system, how the idea was conceived, and the nature of the obstacles placed in the way of even a

[1]Michael Levine, *Fight Back* (New York: Dell Publishing, 1991), p. 4.

modest trial run, casts a revealing light on the real reasons why America's failed drug war continues in full force.

To fully understand the evolution of Fight Back, it is important to understand both my personal and professional stake in our nation's drug problem. In the mid-1980s when the idea first came to me, I had already compiled more than 20 years as a federal narcotics agent. In that time I was directly credited with more than 3,000 arrests and the seizure of several tons of illegal drugs.[2] As a supervisory agent I had overseen at least four times those numbers. I had accomplished all of America's ultimate drug war goals; I had engineered the highest-level sting operations, successfully penetrating the major drug-producing cartels of the world.[3] Yet as all of us who took part in those operations observed, all that we had done at the cost of our lives and families had no effect whatsoever on the streets of the nation we had sworn to serve and protect.

A series of deep cover cases in the 1980s had placed me, posing undercover as a top-level Mafia don, face to face with la Mafia Cruzeña—the Bolivian cocaine cartel—the suppliers of all the raw materials that the Colombian cartels converted into cocaine.[4] I learned that not only did they not fear our war on drugs, they *counted on it* to increase the market price and to weed out the smaller, inefficient drug dealers. They found U.S. interdiction efforts laughable. The only U.S. action they feared was an effective demand reduction program. On one undercover tape-recorded conversation, a top cartel chief, Jorge Roman, expressed his gratitude for the drug war, calling it "a sham put on for the American taxpayer" that was actually "good for business."[5]

Even more dismaying, when I reported Roman's statements to the DEA officer in command of Operation Snowcap (the paramilitary operations begun in South America that Attorney General Edwin Meese had promised would reduce the flow of cocaine to America by 60 percent in three years) he agreed with the drug trafficker, stating, "We know [military operations] don't work, but we sold the

<hr/>

[2]Donald Goddard, *Undercover* (New York: Times Books, 1988), p.13.

[3]Ibid. Levine, *Deep Cover* (New York: Delacorte Press, 1990), p. 17; Michael Levine and Laura Kavanau-Levine, *The Big White Lie* (New York: Thunders Mouth Press, 1993), p. 4.

[4]Ibid. See also Testimony of Felix Milian Rodriguez before U.S. Senate Committee on Foreign Relations, June 25, 1987.

[5]Levine, *Deep Cover*, p. 70.

plan up and down the Potomac. [Snowcap] is going to succeed, one way or the other, or DEA goes down the tubes."[6]

My involvement with family drug problems, if anything, was even closer and more intense than my career exposure. After 20 years on the front lines of the drug war, I was reassigned to New York City as the supervisor of a street enforcement group—a result of a compassionate transfer granted me by DEA due to my 15-year-old daughter's cocaine addiction. My brother David, a heroin addict for 19 years and a graduate of six government-funded treatment-on-demand programs, had previously committed suicide in Miami, leaving a note stating, "I am sorry . . . I can't stand the drugs any longer."[7]

Terrified that my daughter might go the same way as my brother, I was determined to do whatever it took to save her. And now there was a new worry. My son Keith Richard Levine had just become a New York City police officer and on his very first night of duty, in a drug related incident, had come chillingly close to death. A few years later my boy's luck ran out—he was killed in the line of duty by a lifelong drug addict who, like my brother, had been vetted through numerous treatment-on-demand programs. The man, free on parole, had been convicted of two homicides prior to killing my son.

And it wasn't just my family. During my career I had watched the federal drug war budget go from tens of millions to tens of billions, yet the problem throughout the U.S. was worse than ever. I was nearing the end of my career plagued by the notion that it had all been for nothing. With all the expertise I had acquired, could I not at least help find a viable solution before I retired?

The 92nd Street Drug War Blitz

If I had to pick the specific moment when the Fight Back program began to take shape, it was probably on a warm spring evening on the upper West Side of Manhattan. I sat in a black Mercedes sedan, seized months earlier from a drug dealer, with the engine running to keep the A/C going and the salsa music pulsing low and steady.

When a guy wearing a baseball cap knocked on the passenger-side window I jumped, startled. I'd been watching the corner be-

[6]Ibid., p. 81.
[7]Levine, *Fight Back*, p. vii.

hind me, 92nd Street and Amsterdam Avenue, through my rear-view, thinking about the battle that was about to take place there. Months earlier, in drug related incidents, two young cops had been killed on the same night only a few blocks away. One was killed while making an undercover street buy of cocaine, just as I was about to do. My undercover buy was to be the opening salvo of a high-intensity drug enforcement operation begun by the 92nd Street Block Association, a politically active, multi-racial organization of middle to upper income professionals.

One of the association's leaders whom I will call "Vernon" described how the intersection, the heart of the community, was taken over by drug dealers as soon as the sun went down. Area residents became frightened, cowering victims in high-rise caves, fearful of even going to the local store for milk. Years of conventional police action had accomplished nothing. Vernon had contacted Congressman Charles Rangel. The group paid more than its share of drug war taxes; they asked, couldn't anything be done?

Congressman Rangel responded by applying political pressure and demanding action from DEA. That's where I came in. I was placed in charge of a 25-man task force of DEA agents and city detectives. My orders: "Clean up that damned corner, once and for all."

We were able to identify more than 100 probable street dealers within 50 feet of the intersection, servicing an endless flow of customers from dusk till dawn. My agents also learned that during the past several years the local police had made hundreds of dealer arrests at the intersection, yet our eyes didn't lie: Business could not have been better.

Rudolph Giuliani, the then U.S. attorney, assigned one of his assistants to oversee the operation. It was decided that the arrests of the dealers would be done on the basis of simple observations of what appeared to be illegal drug sales, establishing probable cause. We did not have the manpower to use the more traditional measures of undercover buys backed up by surveillance and field investigation, measures that would have made successful prosecution in court more likely. To target the intersection's many potential dealers for arrest, adhering to constitutional and legal safeguards ensuring due process, would have required hundreds of man hours to arrest a single dealer and thousands to convict him. A thousand officers would be needed to police that one single corner, and there were only 250 DEA agents stationed in New York at the time.

This was a typical example of what every professional narcotics officer learns during his or her career but is reluctant to say in public: There is a simple numerical equation that clearly shows that enforcing criminal laws against dealers has about as much chance of making any impact on the drug problem as your Honda Civic has of breaking the sound barrier.

Here's the equation: Number of potential drug dealers *plus* world's potential source countries *divided by* number of narcotics officers and available budget *multiplied by* constitutional legal process to arrest and/or seize *equals:* Total absurdity of U.S. drug war policy.

The prosecutor insisted that the first arrest of the operation be made in the conventional way—an undercover buy/bust—for a good legal reason. A new federal law had just been passed making the sale of drugs within 1,000 feet of a school a "super felony" with a minimum mandatory sentence. This was to be its first prosecution in Manhattan. Giuliani, wanting to make certain that he had a winner and that a message be sent to other dealers, ordered that the undercover agent making the first buy be able to testify that the dealer knew, beyond a reasonable doubt, that he was selling drugs near a school.

Since I was fluent in Spanish—most of the dealers were Dominicans—I decided to make the buy myself. And what better way to prove that the dealer was aware that he was selling dope near a school than to do the transaction parked directly under one of the new signs proclaiming DRUG FREE SCHOOL ZONE.

"You got the money?" he says, getting into my car, showing me a package of white powder. He's a good-looking Dominican kid, early 20s, his eyes darting all over the street alert to every movement.

I read him as typical of the wave of young Dominican "illegals" coming to New York City to make their fortune selling cocaine and returning to their country to buy homes and businesses, marry their childhood sweethearts, and become honored men. The hypocrisy of the drug war—our covert support of drug-dealing political allies, our elected leaders violating the same laws for which thousands of citizens are serving jail time—has made coming to America and getting rich in the drug market, in the view of third world youth, an almost mythical rite of passage, an honorable adventure.

The bag of dope is in his left hand extended toward me; his right hand is out of sight. He's waiting for the money and he doesn't have much patience. Without a word I point to the DRUG FREE SCHOOL ZONE sign, right above the windshield.

The guy laughs and waves his finger at me, "Hey, that don't mean you get the coke for free." I laugh too, hand him the money, and hit my blinkers, the signal for his arrest. He's counting money and doesn't see the guys closing in with guns in their hands.

Sometimes people laugh when I tell the story, but there's nothing funny about it. The law meant less than nothing to the dealer. If the history of the drug war has shown us anything, it is that no matter how draconian the law, drug dealers are not impressed. They have proven themselves, time and again, willing to risk jail and even death for the money. And as every dealer knows, if he is arrested, there are hundreds right behind him ready to take his place. The money is just too good. And like the human wave attacks during the Korean war, the sheer number of dealers, in spite of all laws, has long overtaxed our resources.

It took a squad of 10 men the rest of the night to process the prisoner, run down some leads, write reports, store evidence, seize and inventory his car, question and release for lack of evidence two people who had accompanied him, and put him in a cell. By the following morning we had expended a total of 220 man hours on the case and much of the administrative work, including case reports, was still to be done. The doper was free on bail before we could get home to sleep; he has never been seen since. He joined the huge and growing legion of drug war fugitives that, if all were caught, would now require a prison the size of Rhode Island to house.

Misunderstood Statistics, False Conclusions

One of the most important lessons to be learned from the 92nd Street Operation came during the dealer arrest stage. Within two weeks my task force had made close to 80 dealer arrests, most of which were made on the basis of observations alone. That meant that proving sale of drugs in court was virtually impossible. Any novice lawyer could get a not-guilty verdict, and we all knew it. Thus most of the arrested dealers were only charged with possession.

Of the 10,000-plus narcotics investigations that I have been associated with during my career, 99 percent targeted dealers, not buyers. However, most of the arrested dealers were either charged with, or plea bargained for a possession violation. It is a simple legal expedient that saves time and court costs.

I have heard many experts state that since the highest percentage of jailed drug cases result from possession arrests, the drug war is therefore a "war on drug users." The reason drug war bureaucrats and politicians usually don't even respond to this accusation is that it could not be further from the truth; yet the notion persists. Many drug war bureaucrats are happy to hear the false claim repeated over and over in the media, because it acts to discredit much of the otherwise credible drug war opposition and helps maintain the status quo. An interesting statistic proves my point: According to DEA, 85 percent of drug consumers are white. My personal experience puts the figure closer to 90 percent. If the drug war was truly being waged against consumers, those statistics would be reflected in jail populations, but they are not.

Some experts continue to misunderstand the racially unbalanced jail populations of those incarcerated for drug violations, making a blanket claim that the drug war somehow targets minorities instead of whites. While recognizing that unfortunately racism does exist in law enforcement as it does in much of the rest of today's society, those on the inside of narcotics enforcement know that this is not the predominant reason for the disparity in jail population. Rather, it is more directly connected to our philosophy of focusing the majority of our law enforcement efforts on arresting suppliers and dealers, the majority of whom happen to be minorities. This is true for a combination of economic, linguistic, and cultural reasons combined with ill advised immigration policies.

The 92nd Street campaign was typical of street narcotics enforcement in urban America. For a couple of days we succeeded in sharply reducing the appearance of a drug market, mainly because the police activity frightened off the buyers; however, within a week of our departure "Vernon" called me with bad news. The drug dealers, in many cases the same people whom we had arrested, were on the street selling again. It was as if we had never even been there. The father of two preteen daughters was at his wits' end. "If all those cops and agents couldn't get this one corner clean, what is the purpose of this whole damned drug war?" he asked. "You're a DEA agent; can you explain it to me?"

I was as desperate for an answer as he was.[8]

Why Does the Drug War Continue?

I began to do something I had never done before: Examine the mechanics of our war on drugs and the motivation of those pursu-

[8]Levine, *Fight Back*, p. 26.

ing it, including my own. I used classic investigative reasoning, asking the question: Who benefits most from a continued war on drugs?

I found a quote by Brooks Atkinson that seemed to resonate: "Bureaucracies are designed to perform public business. But as soon as a bureaucracy is established, it develops an autonomous spiritual life and comes to regard the public as its enemy."

The trillion dollar war on drugs then included 53 federal, military, law enforcement, and covert agencies; the Partnership for a Drug Free America and all its branches; and treatment-on-demand programs—just for starters. That wasn't even counting state agencies that came under separate budgets like New York State, which, on Governor Mario Cuomo's watch at the time, had its own drug war budget of one billion dollars.

It brought to mind how DEA agents would joke whenever mainstream media would headline some new statistic showing that we were winning: "Please! Not yet," someone would cry. "I've got a mortgage to pay." One DEA administrator in response to media-trumpeted claims, used to address audiences of agents with, "I guess we've 'turned the corner' again." Some agent would always respond: "Yeah, we've squared the block."[9]

The point is that none of these bureaucracies even consider the possibility of successfully completing their goals. On the contrary they all vie with each other for bigger cases, better headlines, and more media exposure, which translate to a bigger cut of the budget, more money, more authority, and more power. The notion of really winning the drug war is so far out of the question that anyone who even mentions it is considered some kind of a nut. Perhaps there are some individuals inside the drug war who sincerely wish for that victory, but nobody really believes it's possible. And to say publicly what is secretly felt by every insider—that if the federal war on drugs were disbanded tomorrow it would make little difference on any street in America—would be like invoking the Antichrist. It would be a threat to the existence of the bureaucracy, to countless careers, and to the benefits, money, and security they provide at taxpayer expense.

Mainstream Media: A Key Beneficiary of the War

The fourth estate, the national news media, which our founding fathers believed to be absolutely necessary to safeguard our democ-

[9]Levine, *Fight Back*, p. 1.

racy, must shoulder their share of the responsibility. The majority of us cannot accept that the drug war is a total failure mainly because the mainstream media have done such a successful job of selling it to us.

The decades-long manipulation of media by bureaucrats to sell a failed, inept government policy is nothing new. For example, it is now evident that, through much of the buildup of the Vietnam war, mainstream media, with just a few exceptions, dutifully headlined false intelligence estimates, battle statistics, and body counts announced by America's political and military leaders, and without a minimal amount of investigation. This false information blitz kept us bleeding, dying, and paying for a victory that never came. The media then tagged insiders who tried to tell the truth with the pejorative "whistleblower," or worse, portrayed them as anti-American. For many years it convinced a majority of us, including me, at the time a young federal agent working undercover in Southeast Asia, to pay no attention to mounting evidence of the lies of our military and political leaders appearing in alternative media. If it's not in the *New York Times* it can't be true, can it?

The drug war is now running an exact parallel to our Vietnam experience. In fact our military involvement in places like Bolivia, Colombia, and Peru, under the banner of War on Drugs, continues to be increasingly funded and expanded to the point that some members of Congress have recently described them as leading us into "another Vietnam-type debacle."[10] Yet most mainstream media continue to respond to manipulation by bureaucrats by ignoring this frightening forecast.

Throughout my career I have observed and, regrettably, taken part in what can only be described as the ongoing unhealthy alliance between drug war and mainstream media bureaucracies. When I was stationed in New York City, for example, all the major networks and newspapers would call the DEA special agent in charge when, due to a slow news week, they *needed* a drug story for ratings or to sell newspapers. The agent was always eager to comply because the request was always beneficial to the agency's image and budget, not to mention his own career. Dramatic raids reported in media, like the best in Madison Avenue advertising, helped sell the drug war.

My unit, a very active street enforcement group, was often called

[10]George Gedda, "GOP Sees Colombia as Another Vietnam," Associated Press, August 6, 1999.

upon to plan drug raids for the benefit of mainstream media cameras. Often this would entail the disruption of undeveloped investigations to meet media deadlines and, at times, the use of dangerous, unprofessional tactics for dramatic effect, as happened with ATF's infamous Waco raid.

Of course, a kind of "don't ask" policy was in effect: The journalists involved would never ask an embarrassing question of the agency. But they had to be hopelessly naive to accept at face value the likelihood that DEA, FBI, ATF, or any of the other drug war bureaucracy they approached for a story, just happened to have a dramatic, action-filled case ready to be filmed in time for their deadline. The unspoken complicity of government and press was as cynical as it was sinister.

If a particular journalist dared to question the authenticity of what was happening, the next time he came to the agency for a story he'd run into a brick wall. He would get nothing. Thus if a network or newspaper journalist wanted continued access to any federal drug war agency, he or she had better be friendly.

During the heat of the 1992 presidential campaign "Operation Green Ice" was called the biggest international money-laundering case in history by every major media outlet in America. While it was being featured everywhere from "Larry King Live" to "Geraldo," I was getting angry calls from Customs and DEA agents who had actually participated in the case.

The frustrated and enraged federal agents, who knew I would protect their identities, told me that the case was a fraud. The White House, through the Justice Department, had ordered Customs and DEA to come up with a series of major international arrests to "prove" that the Bush administration was making drug war "gains." Thus, many agents were ordered to prematurely shut down major money-laundering investigations so that their individual cases could be falsely included in a worldwide, headline grabbing roundup—"Operation Green Ice." It would be described by American politicians through our ever-compliant media as "the best example of international cooperation" in the drug war, when, in fact, according to my sources, it was nothing more than a hodgepodge of hastily drawn indictments and unrelated arrest warrants linked together to "bust" an international drug conspiracy that never existed.[11]

[11]Michael Levine, "Who Will Finally Tell the People?" *Extra*, March 1993.

Ironically, I had just been invited to make a presentation in Paris by the French government–sponsored Geopolitical Drug Watch. Phillippe Bordes, a French journalist, approached me. He wanted to talk about, of all things, "Operation Green Ice." What did I think of it? He told me that French police had refused to take part in it, calling it an "obvious fraud." French law enforcement officials warned that if the American Justice Department persisted in trying to include them, they would blow the whistle on them in the French media.[12]

Media Drug Money?

Perhaps the worst example of the mutual vested interest in a permanent drug war among bureaucracies and mainstream media occurred in November 1998, when President Clinton and Newt Gingrich raised each other's hands in bipartisan "victory" and awarded an unprecedented $2 billion to mainstream media for yet another antidrug ad campaign, making the Partnership for a Drug Free America one of the biggest advertisers on Madison Avenue.

In my book *Fight Back,* published in 1991, I cited detailed research indicating that antidrug ads were not only ineffective but that there was much evidence that they were counterproductive, and, further, that this sentiment was echoed by educators across the land.[13] *Brand Week,* the leading advertising trade magazine, in a scathing commentary against the costly federal ad campaign, called it "suspect." Yet mainstream media had no comment. A cynical ex–federal agent might ask, Why would they comment when they are the beneficiaries?

I attended a movie theater recently where one of these expensively produced, antidrug ads was shown before the feature presentation—a Disney Studios release. It featured the story of a young black boy named "Kevin" who was forced to run home over backyard fences to escape drug dealers, whom the narrator said, "would not take 'no' for an answer." The trouble with this message is that, as every kid knows, and as a Reagan Administration survey proved, virtually 100 percent of kids get their first hard drug experience *free* from their friends.

Teenagers in the theater snickered at the million dollar-plus ad.

[12]Ibid.
[13]Levine, *Fight Back,* p. 163.

What the kids know apparently a lot better than the Partnership for a Drug Free America who produced the ad, is that drug dealers don't come looking for customers; it is the other way around. And, as the article in *Brand Week* pointed out, Disney Studios was the recipient of the first $60 million of taxpayer-funded ad money.

In the August 29th edition of the *New York Times*, there was a full page, $50,000 ad, again sponsored by the Partnership for a Drug Free America, called "How to Plan a Funeral for Your 12-Year-Old Son." It almost drove *me* to drugs. The offensive ad ended with, "If you don't want to learn about funerals, learn about sniffing." Does anyone really believe that this message will keep a single kid off drugs? What really hurts is that there are effective but severely underfunded community groups that are successfully saving lives who could have used the $50,000 to fund their activities for many years.[14]

The real irony about the $2 billion antidrug media blitz hit home when I received a phone call from a distraught DEA agent who still believed that stopping the supply was the solution. He told me that according to DEA's own statistics, the money could have been used to purchase every single coca leaf grown in South America that year, and then some.

And it was no surprise to me when *USA Today*, in its August 16, 1999, edition, published front-page headlines trumpeting a statistical decrease in the use of drugs as "turning the corner"—an endorsement of the $2 billion ad campaign as money well spent. How could this be honest reporting when it failed to mention that precisely this same statistical victory claim had been made repeatedly for three decades? If *USA Today* checked its own archives, it would find that drug czar William Bennett retired in "victory" eight years ago on the wings of just such a claim.

Recently, as happens often, a mainstream media journalist contacted me for a comment on a breaking story about the Mexican drug war. Apparently he had uncovered yet more evidence of Mexican government drug corruption constituting, he said, "a serious threat to America."

He had no comment when I pointed out that Congress had just granted Mexico "cooperating nation" status in the drug war. I told him that if he looked back over the past 25 years in the archives of

[14]*New York Times*, August 29, 1999.

his own newspaper, he would find the same pro forma, Mexican drug war story printed almost bimonthly. The only thing that changed was the name of the current Mexican Dr. Evil, amounts, and dates. The syntax, adjectives, and text were the same. The reporter was writing a fill-in-the-blanks drug story. He didn't need my opinion, just a copy machine.

Incredible as it seems, I have documented the same formula drug stories printed beneath American newspaper headlines dating back 80 years![15] What the mainstream media do not realize, or do not want to realize, is that while the repetitious drug war "victory" story sells newspapers and gets rating points, it also sells a deadly and wasteful drug war to an all-too gullible American public. If the Fourth Estate won't tell America that its drug war is broken beyond all repair, who will?

The really big question that remains is this: If by some miracle we can get the nation to agree that the war on drugs is a failure, do we have a viable alternative solution to the problem?

Is Legalization a Solution?

As most of us with firsthand experience with hard drugs believe, blanket legalization is more a threat than a solution. Especially to those of us who have loved ones at risk of addiction. Certain soft drugs may be legalized with a downside no worse than alcohol, but I am convinced that the hard stuff like crack, coke, heroin, angel dust, methamphetamine, LSD, ecstasy, and dozens of others simply cannot be legalized in a sane society.

A poll taken by the Bush administration indicated that more than 90 percent of those children who grow up in ghettos and who, through some miracle of willpower, resist peer pressure and never take hard drugs, gave as their first reason for resisting, that drugs are *illegal.* Tell the father of one of these young heros that you want to make hard drugs legal and watch out you don't get punched in the face.

Hard drugs, in my long experience, are relentlessly addictive and life-destroying, while alcohol, as damaging as it is in a small percentage of its buyers, is a long-accepted rite of passage that is in most cases survivable. And while Peter Bourne, President Carter's

[15]Gary Silver and Michael Aldrich, ed., *The Dope Chronicles* (New York: Harper and Row, 1979), p. 105.

drug advisor, was proclaiming cocaine "the most benign of the illegal drugs," Michael Baden, New York City's medical examiner, was pointing out before an audience of DEA agents and New York City detectives that "cocaine, 80 percent of our hard-core drug problem, is a poison that kills directly by attacking every vital organ of the body."[16] Only street-wise narcotics officers heard Dr. Baden's words, while the world media trumpeted the false proclamation of the White House drug expert.

Not only is there no real comparison between hard drugs and alcohol but the majority of our society does not want hard drugs legalized and has said so loud and clear in every poll—and for good reason.

What happened in Russia during the past decade seems to emphasize the point. Before glasnost, when the use of hard drugs was a serious criminal offense, Russia maintained a hard-core addict population of fewer than 110,000. As a result of glasnost, the use of drugs was decriminalized. It is expected now that by the year 2000 Russia will have more than 7 million hard-core addicts.

Even the experts who call for blanket legalization do not have convincing answers for obvious questions such as: How would you handle the sale and/or distribution of drugs like crack, now estimated to be responsible for 60 percent of all crime? Angel dust? Heroin? LSD? Who would be allowed to sell and/or distribute hard drugs and to whom? How would prices be regulated? What about advertising campaigns? Would there be an age cutoff? And if there is an age cutoff, who would enforce those laws and how? If we gave away drugs like crack, cocaine, and heroin free of charge, would the addicts then stop committing crimes? What could a strung-out crack addict who needs to toot up every 15 minutes do for a living? What do we do with the projected increase in crack babies? Is it not proven that some of these drugs, like crack, in themselves induce violence? Since we know that cocaine is a poison, how do we handle the massive medical costs legalization would bring? What about lawsuits against the manufacturers of hard drugs like those brought against tobacco companies?

Typical responses show that not much thought has been given toward the reality of what would actually happen in our society.

---

[16]Series of conferences given by Dr. Baden at DEA headquarters in NYC, during the late 1970s.

Most experts seem to support legalization in the abstract. The fact is, blanket legalization creates as many problems as it solves.

A recent paradox in the debate over legalization is that many of the same people calling for the legalization of hard drugs are now calling for the prohibition of tobacco. Go figure.

Is Treatment a Solution?

There are two kinds of treatment—treatment on demand and mandatory treatment. Virtually all funding goes toward treatment on demand. I have never seen the question of the efficacy of treatment on demand answered more directly and with more impact than in a *Washington Post* article titled "Treatment on Demand: The Mythology" by Richard Moran, a professor of sociology and criminology at Mount Holyoke College.[17]

Professor Moran argued that in spite of 1.4 million taxpayer-paid treatment-on-demand slots reserved for hard-core addicts, the Clinton administration was about to spend $335 million to create an additional 140,000 slots, and that all of it was doomed to fail. Moran contended that the whole theory of 'treatment-on-demand' rests on three unproved and highly doubtful assumptions:

Assumption 1: That heavy drug buyers want to be treated. Unfortunately this assumption goes against the weight of evidence. Despite the constant increase of "Treatment on Demand" programs, the number of hard-core addicts, 2.7 million, has remained constant for 15 years. A National Institute on Drug Abuse study on the spread of HIV found that almost half of all drug addicts who had been on hard drugs for more than 15 years had never been on any treatment whatsoever, not even detoxification. For them the dreadful reality is that drug addiction is a way of life that no political rhetoric, pleading, or ad campaign will ever change.

Assumption 2: That drug treatment is not available. The 1.4 million slots already available, using the average residential program length of nine months would indicate that all known addicts could undergo treatment within an 18-month period. Professor Moran pointed out that there were long waiting lists here and there, and needs and available programs do not always coincide. Nonetheless, most programs still operate below capacity. An addict who requests

[17]Richard Moran, "Treatment on Demand: The Mythology," *Washington Post*, April 19, 1994.

treatment is often on as many as 10 waiting lists, thus creating the mistaken impression that drug addicts are clamoring to get into current treatment programs.

The truth is that many addicts . . . have been in and out of treatment all their lives. In a Western Massachusetts drug detoxification clinic, for example, the average addict has been treated more than 200 times. My own brother had been through at least six treatment programs.

Assumption 3: Treatment is effective in eliminating long-term drug use. As Professor Moran concluded, the statistics show that hardcore addiction is all but impossible to treat, and certainly not on an 'on-demand' basis. Indeed research from the National Institute on Drug Abuse study suggests that hard-core drug addiction runs its course in about 15 years, whether or not treatment is provided. Without adequate knowledge of how to treat heavy drug buyers, adding more treatment slots will turn out to be a colossal waste of time and money.

Given that treatment-on-demand programs are a statistically proven failure, it is sobering to note that whole massive treatment bureaucracies and industries, depending on a steady flow of addicts for their income, have now proliferated throughout the United States. For example, the director of Phoenix House, one of the largest, nonprofit, treatment-on-demand programs, himself an exaddict, was earning a salary in the high six figures. When I began my research on the Fight Back program and interviewed a woman answering a cocaine hot line, she confided that she had been told by her supervisors that every incoming call was worth a potential $17,000.

The Chinese Cure

I found the first clue leading me toward the Fight Back solution in a statement made in 1975 by Congressman Charles Rangel on the floor of Congress: "When the People's Republic of China eradicated [its drug addiction problem] the United States took no notice of that significant fact. This was a reflection of our foreign policy of pretending that they did not even exist."[18]

Those words started me on an incredible journey of discovery that continues to this day. I, like most Americans, believed that China solved its massive drug problem by executing all the people

---

[18]Rep. Charles Rangel (D-N.Y.), *Congressional Record*, October 6, 1975, E5261.

who wouldn't quit. In fact, that is what I still hear experts alleging to this day. Yet when I researched the facts, I was astounded to find out that this too, like the arrest and treatment statistics, could not have been farther from the truth.

At the end of World War II, China had a staggering 70 million heroin and opium addicts. When Mao Tse-Tung's army conquered mainland China in 1949, priority was the suppression of *drug addiction*—not a war against drug supply or dealers.

All hard-core addicts were required to undergo treatment or be forcibly interned in a treatment center until cured. The program was accompanied by antidrug *consumer* propaganda. The drug consumer was depicted as the enemy, the culprit who fueled the drug economy and without whom there would be no demand. The enemy yes, but a redeemable one who could reinvent himself by rehabilitation. In other words, China was going to save and redeem the addicts whether they liked it or not.

The result of the program was that by spring of 1951, less than two years after its inception, the New China News Agency announced that China's drug problem of 70 million addicts was "fundamentally eradicated."[19] Compare this with the 2.7 million estimated hard-core addicts we now have, buying an estimated 80 percent of hard drugs. Were there executions? Yes, during the three years of the antinarcotics campaign there were 27 executions of dealers—clearly not the reason for their success.

The Japanese Cure

Japan's drug problem was at its height in 1963 when that country decided to follow China's approach and passed a drug law that included mandatory commitment of drug buyers to mental hospitals. This was accompanied by a Chinese-style propaganda campaign vilifying drug users as the destroyers of a safe, sane society. It became the duty of each community to aid in the identification and rehabilitation of its own users. In less than three years the Japanese were as successful as the Chinese. In a study of Japan's success, Masamutsu Nagahama, chief of the Narcotics Section, Ministry of Health and Welfare, said, "We think we can state that the

[19]Martin B. Margulis, "China Has No Drug Problem—Why?" *Parade* magazine, October 15, 1972; Shen Chenrv, "Keeping Narcotics Under Strict Control: Some Effects on China," *Impact on Science and Society*, No. 133, 1984; Albert P. Blaustein, ed., *Fundamental Legal Documents of Communist China* (South Hackensack, N.J.: Fred R. Rothman & Company, 1962), pp. 237–239.

drug problem is under control, thanks to the strong line taken to eradicate *addiction*."[20]

My first thought after reading about the solutions chosen by China and Japan was that, if we had had an Americanized version of what these two ancient cultures did instead of our war on drugs, my brother and son would be alive today, as would the millions who have perished in this longest war in American history.

Implications of the Asian Solutions

Having grown up in the South Bronx in the '50s, it occurred to me that the image of the heroin addict in the United States during those innocent years was similar to the socially unacceptable images projected by the Asian authorities during their cures. In the 1950s in America, an addict was seen as a lowlife and a felon, someone despicable who lay in your hallway urinating on himself. The image was very effective in keeping city kids off drugs. Not very PC. I know, I was one of those kids. It was certainly a far cry from the image of today's addict, which includes supermodels, athletes, and movie stars who do Partnership for a Drug Free America "say no" television ads between arrests and visits to the Betty Ford Clinic.

In the 1960s, the image of the addict began to change. The learned among us suddenly understood how unhappiness or a dysfunctional family life could lead a hapless person to lose his will to say "no" and become a victim of drugs. My baby brother fell for the hype at age 15 and paid for it with 19 years of heroin addiction and ultimately suicide.

I've rarely heard an addict explain why he started hard drugs, without reciting, parrot-like, the psychological and socioeconomic reasons heard on national television and radio shows. It was either the Medellin Cartel, Manny Noriega, their poor economic condition, their too affluent economic condition, corrupt police, or their father's fault. And if you don't believe me, just read the news.

The image of today's addict, a victim of drugs, a person of no willpower who if confronted with drugs must take them, is as damaging to the addict as it is to the community. Has the Medellin

[20]Levine, *Fight Back*, p. 15. See also "How Japan Solved Its Drug Problem," *Readers Digest*, June 1973; "A Review of Drug Abuse and Countermeasures in Japan since WWII," *Bulletin in Narcotics*, Vol. 20, No. 3, July–September 1968; Professor Hiroshi Kumagi, "Drug Abuse and Countermeasures in Japan," *Medical Journal*, Malaysia, December 1974.

Cartel really victimized us, as New York's mayor Edward Koch once indicated in national headlines when he called for the retaliatory bombing of Colombia? Or are our drug problems really the fault of a policy that tells us it is the government's responsibility to stop the flow of drugs. And that the addict is a hapless victim?

According to most psychologists, our "stop the drugs" policy could not be more damaging to those at risk. It is called enabling. The message we should be giving our children is that no matter how many illegal drugs are available, they have the will to refuse. It is a choice. By placing personal responsibility back on the users, society becomes primed for a new solution to this deadly problem.

Fight Back Is Conceived

Drugs are a business. The American way of business competition focuses on demand. Supply follows demand, not vice versa as the drug war bureaucrats claim. Discourage buyers and the dealers go out of business.

Throughout my career I observed that wherever there was an obvious police presence, no matter how bad the community, drug buyers would vanish like smoke on a windy day. If the police presence was maintained long enough, dealers would shut down and move on. Suppliers and dealers, on the other hand, protected by high-priced lawyers and enticed by huge and growing profits, were impossible to frighten away. If we in America would focus all our enforcement and rehabilitation resources on the buyer in an American-style cure, I believed the battle would be won as quickly as it was in Japan and China.

I found evidence all over the country, of individual communities whose aggressively vocal and visible presence on the street going after "johns" to combat prostitution was 100 percent effective. Why not apply the same tactics to drugs? I looked further and found communities that, without funding or police support, were effective in stopping drug trafficking by frightening away the buyers.[21]

Buyers, 85% of whom are so-called casual users with jobs, homes, and families to protect, can be frightened by almost anything. If they spot a police car, a camera, someone who looks like a cop, an angry citizen staring at them, they move on. Hard-core buyers, most of

[21]Levine, *Fight Back*, p. 54.

whom live from fix to fix, are terrified of losing their drugs to police seizures. Many are fugitives and repeat offenders responsible for numerous drug related crimes. All buyers live in fear of being identified.

If an area was considered hot by the buyers—watched by the police—drug business died instantly. I therefore began the Fight Back plan by listing various step-by-step tactics that citizens, working in partnership with police, might use to create a zone that is hostile for drug buyers.[22]

Yes, they would move elsewhere, but it would disrupt business entirely, which always acts to lessen all drug related crime. What would happen if the national focus of all those billions of dollars were on illegal drug buyers? There would be no "elsewhere."

Targeting Buyers and the Constitution

Among the early, unfounded fears expressed about the Fight Back program was that it might be unconstitutional. On the contrary, among the plan's primary intentions was the rescuing of our already drug-war shredded constitutional protections against illegal search and seizure, violations of privacy without due process, the taking of citizens' lives by police in violation of the rules of engagement, and punishment that is disproportionate to the crime committed.

A poll taken during the Bush administration indicating that 60 percent of Americans were willing to give up rights under the Constitution to win our supply-side drug war, seemed to some to give government a mandate to take those rights. As a federal narcotics agent and now a defense consultant and expert witness, I am a firsthand witness to the myriad of constitutional abuses committed in the name of the drug war.

Another concern expressed was that it seemed unfair to target the "little guy"; that is, the drug consumer. My answer is that if you had seen the damage done to communities where I lived and worked by dollars deposited there by the "little guy," you might think differently. His dollars buy the bullets that kill kids only feet from where he satisfies his need for illegal drugs. As painful as it is for those of us who have loved ones who are drug buyers, we must recognize that it is their dollars that fuel the entire world drug economy. A

[22]Ibid., p. 49.

high percentage of all crime, including the majority of national ho-micides, is drug-related.[23]

Would We Fill the Jails With Consumers?

Absolutely not. "Targeting buyers" means dissuading the major-ity of them from buying illegal drugs by any legal means, with jail as a last resort. Jail terms for most buyers, with the exception of violent criminals, is neither desirable nor necessary. In fact, if we changed our focus from supply to illegal drug buyers, there would instantly be a drastic reduction in jail populations.

The reduced market would mean that far few dealers would be arrested. And most illegal drug buyers would not have to be pro-cessed through the courts at all. A non-violent buyer can be handled noncriminally, with a large fine and/or seizure of his vehicle, for example. Violent and/or armed offenders caught with drugs—like the man who killed my son and two other people—would be pros-ecuted for possession and placed in jail where they could not con-tinue to damage the innocents around them. Hard-core addicts with long arrest records for nonviolent crimes in support of their habit, will be offered mandatory treatment in lieu of jail; that is, they will be given the opportunity to get off hard drugs or face jail for the crime they committed. And if they learned a productive trade in the process, we could save their lives whether they liked it or not.

The 109th Street Experiment

As a DEA supervisory agent assigned to New York City, I was in a perfect position to isolate one of the worst drug-infested streets in our nation and run a field test to ascertain whether simply changing the enforcement focus from dealers to buyers would work as effec-tively as I had theorized. In March of 1989, two years before my retirement, a typical *New York Times* drug war article aimed me at Fight Back's first field test.

The article called the area of 109th Street between Amsterdam and Columbus Avenue the worst drug-dealing block in the city, com-plete with murderous gangs and numerous crack houses. Thou-

---

[23]Michael Levine, *Deep Cover*, p. 215 and *Fight Back*, p. 96; Michael Levine and Laura Kavanau, *The Big White Lie*, p. 5.

sands of dealer arrests had been made in the area over a several-year period, yet the drug business had never been healthier.[24]

With a 12-to-15-man squad, I planned to target the area's buyers exclusively and, for the time being, to leave the dealers alone. I knew I didn't have a chance approaching U.S. Attorney Rudolph Giuliani for authorization for the operation. At the time, the smallest seizure case the federal court would accept was one kilo of cocaine—typical of our get-the-dealer policy.[25]

Instead I contacted Manhattan Special Prosecutor Sterling Johnson, who has since been named a federal judge. His first thought was that I wanted to arrest drug consumers and prosecute them in the already clogged Manhattan Criminal Court system. I explained that my intention was merely to frighten the buyers with an arrest but not follow through with a prosecution unless the person detained was a violent criminal. I wanted to see what effect simply frightening the buyer would have on this worst of all drug dealing blocks in Manhattan. Prosecutor Johnson authorized the operation.

For the next several weeks my squad set up an ambush of drug buyers at the most active dealing location on the block, a two-sided basement.[26] Every night a line of cars double-parked in front of the location, backed up at times half way down the block, with customers running in and out making buys of cocaine, crack, and heroin. As buyers would drive off, we performed a classic "angeling off" operation. We followed them a distance away from the dealer, pulled them over, searched their cars and arrested them.

Most turned out to be white professionals—teachers, lawyers, salesmen, stockbrokers, etc.—from outside the community as far away as Massachusetts. Most were completely bowled over by the experience of the arrest, pleading for a second chance, terrified of being exposed. All signed statements identifying the dealers in the basement. Most were eventually released with the warning that, from then on, all buyers coming onto that block would be arrested. My hope was that they would pass the word on to others. The few exceptions who were jailed were hard-core addicts with long criminal records, some of whom were armed fugitives. What was appar-

---

[24]Selwyn Raab, "Brutal Gangs Wage War of Terror in Upper Manhattan," *New York Times*, March 15, 1989.

[25]Levine, *Fight Back*, p. 31.

[26]For a full description of the operation, see Michael Levine, *Fight Back*, p. 28.

ent was that if the vast majority of these buyers had thought that there was even a possibility of arrest or identification they never would have been out there buying illegal drugs in the first place.

For the next several days we continued "angeling off" buyers, identifying more dealers, collecting more statements and descriptions, spreading the word that buyers were being targeted. The operation continued from March 23 to March 30, 1989, during which time *all* drug business in the neighborhood—about two square blocks—was reduced to a trickle. It was an unusual scene for us. Dealers, for the first time, came out of the basement and stood right in front of us peering up and down the streets wondering what could have possibly happened to their customers.

On the night of March 30, armed with search and arrest warrants for the dealers, we raided the basement and found it abandoned. Of course they had probably moved their operation to another location with less heat. What if this were a national policy, instead of the "stop drugs and dealers" policy that has failed for three decades? It was well over a year before the drug business began trickling back into the neighborhood, but at nowhere near the prior levels; the buyers were still largely frightened. I was certain that if we had been able to keep the heat on the buyers using a trained citizens' group, the neighborhood would have remained completely drug free.

Thus, I began writing *Fight Back*, the detailed, step-by-step fight plan for communities and police to maintain a permanent street pressure on drug demand. Of course nothing was guaranteed, but, living in a nation where the drug economy was causing war-like casualties on our streets and where everything else seemed doomed to failure, it certainly seemed worth a try.

Fight Back Plan of Action (short outline version)[27]

1. Community and police are educated to the realities of supply and demand in the drug business, to counter three decades of media and bureaucracy selling of a supply-side drug war as the Holy Grail. This should include a community media campaign.

2. Community members are trained by police to identify drug-dealing locations in their midst and, remaining in radio contact with police, become a visible deterrent to drug consumers entering the community.

[27]Levine, *Fight Back,* pp. 37–48.

3. Buyers of illegal drugs would be warned by signs and large placards that it is *they* who are targeted. They would be reminded that it is their money that attracts dealers and buys the bullets that kill children in the community; that if they do not heed the warning, they will be arrested for possession of drugs. That police are now secretly surveilling their marketplace, and that it is they who will end up testifying against the dealer who sells them drugs.

4. Community members will be trained in other visible deterrent methods, such as bullhorns, spotlights, video-cameras, etc., and other techniques listed in *Fight Back*—the same methods being used effectively by communities against prostitution "johns" to create a "circle of fear" that will, as experience has proven, frighten away most buyers.

5. Plainclothes police, with community participation as spotters, begin on a selective basis to confront buyers, seizing drugs and ticketing those with no record of violence for future court appearances and fines. A few actions like this will be necessary to give "teeth" to the community-presence deterrent effect.

6. Community courts and prosecutors will work with the Fight Back program. The projections indicate that such a program will lessen court loads substantially. Community members will be encouraged to be present at all proceedings that affect community safety.

7. Mandatory treatment centers where vocational training and education would be provided will be set up as an alternative to jail sentences for nonviolent, crime-committing, hard-core addicts. An addict will be allowed to plead guilty to the crime and will be released into treatment with the understanding that if he returns to hard drugs, he will finish his full sentence.

8. Politically, the community would vote only for those politicians supporting a Fight Back type program.

9. Neighboring communities will join together in the program, policing each other's neighborhoods, in many cases crossing racial lines and knocking down old barriers of misunderstanding.

10. Police-community partnerships will be set up in such a way as to make police corruption and brutality all but impossible. Police will work the community as partners, not an invading force as is typical today.

Greenville, Mississippi

In 1992, a short time after *Fight Back* was published, Sergeant Kirby Slaton of the Greenville, Mississippi, Police Department contacted me. Greenville, a small city on the banks of the Mississippi River, had the third highest crime rate in the South and most of it was drug related. Businesses were closing down and moving elsewhere. More and more citizens were buying and carrying guns to protect their homes and families. Sergeant Slaton and his new chief of police, desperate for a solution, wanted to give Fight Back a try. Would I be willing to come down and help start the program?

A couple of weeks later I was in Greenville speaking to various groups of local citizens. They loved the idea, wanted to get started as soon as possible. I next spoke at all high schools in the inner city, the epicenter of the problem, telling the kids that from that moment on they could look forward to their community video-taping them as they bought illegal drugs. I warned that the police would be setting traps to catch drug buyers. I told them that by spending their money buying dope, they were paying for the very bullets that were killing their little brothers and sisters.

The first reports from street informants indicated that the threat alone had made the buyers paranoid, seeing people behind every window video-taping them. The drug business had all but disappeared from the streets.

When Sergeant Slaton took me to the airport a week later, I thought that we had witnessed the beginning of a change in drug war focus that would finally make an impact. Citizens were volunteering in droves and the police were gearing up to train them as their partners. A community Fight Back video was made and distributed. The effects were already visible on every corner in Greenville.

Weeks later I was shocked to hear that Sergeant Slaton was about to resign. The Justice Department was pressuring Greenville to end or alter the Fight Back program to be more "get the dealer" oriented. The community's "interference" had interrupted "important" federal investigations of dealers. By the citizen volunteers interrupting the dealers' business on the streets, the feds couldn't gather enough probable cause to arrest them. The police finally surrendered to federal and political pressure to change Fight Back to a "drop a dime on the dealer" type program. The Fight Back citizens group became like any other citizens group in the country. Their energy and focus was again aimed at reporting dealers to the police and was having no effect whatsoever on the drug business in their midst.

Another citizens group that started a Fight Back style program in

Natchez, Mississippi, suffered a similar fate. One in Sacramento, California, was met with outright antagonism by police and federal officials. It became clear that Fight Back was threatening to the myriad of bureaucracies that depended on their funding for a continued, no-change war on dealers and supply. It seemed that Fight Back was doomed to disappear—because it was simply too effective.

Cape Cod Experiment

In January, 1992, a month after my son, NYPD Sergeant Keith Richard Levine became the third man in New York City to be killed by a crack addict during the commission of a robbery, I was contacted by Sheriff Jack Demillo of Cape Cod, Massachusetts. The sheriff, a Vietnam veteran and clinical psychologist, had studied the Fight Back program and was enthusiastic about its new, commonsense approach. He wanted to hire me as his drug information bureau director, in an effort to begin the program in his jurisdiction. I would later be referred to by the Massachusetts press as Cape Cod's "drug czar."

My job was similar to that of all the federal drug czars in that it gave me no police powers. The Fight Back program required a full partnership between police and community to succeed. After a year of solid effort I was unable to elicit any police cooperation whatsoever. In fact, DEA agents who were aware of the program confided to me that pressure was being brought to bear on police *not* to cooperate. Just as happened in Greenville, local police were told by the Justice Department and state police, that the citizens' involvement would "interfere" with drug dealer investigations. Ironic, but true. Fight Back, if it worked, would so badly damage the dealers' business that the feds and locals could not arrest them for drug dealing; they would simply close down.

I was successful in getting widespread involvement of the community; building an organization that was ready to go into action; training many of the members myself; designing a visible logo, T-shirts, and hats; and setting up a headquarters with telecommunications and faxes enabling instant communications with local police, yet not a single police agency would work with the citizens.

I tried in every way to obtain the local Partnership for a Drug Free America's support to at least get a trial run of this promising—and proven—program. They had the political and police connections necessary to bring it together. I was totally unsuccessful. Then in an ironic twist of fate, I was accidentally put on the distribution list for one of the Partnership's in-house memos reporting on the minutes of a meeting as follows: "Meeting began with a discussion of the Fight Back program. Both pro and con thoughts were expressed including that 'If Fight Back is successful, it could take the wind out of the sails of the Partnership.'"[28] Their real concern was the same as that of all the other drug war funded bureaucracies: that the Fight Back program might put them out of business.

Of course I never got their support and soon resigned from my position. My unfortunate experience with Fight Back has not changed to date. It seems to threaten too many vested interests, from law enforcement bureaucracies and federally funded rehabilitation programs to covert agencies and drug education programs, for it ever to get a fair trial.

It is too easy for our bureaucrats and media to refuse to look at the methodology behind China's unparalleled and rapid success in ending a drug addiction problem many times worse than ours. But it must be mentioned here that one of the greatest influences on American military strategy was the Chinese military strategist Sun Tzu, whose *The Art of War*, written an estimated 3,500 years ago, is studied at West Point. As Sun Tzu pointed out: "There has never been a protracted war from which a country has benefited."

Perhaps our nation has finally suffered enough under the yoke of the longest, costliest, and deadliest war in its history. Perhaps it is ready to try a new idea. Call Fight Back heresy if you wish, but it has shown it can do better than the current failed war on drugs. The opposition of the entrenched war on drugs bureaucracy attests to that.

[28]"Minutes of Marketing Task Force" of the Cape and Islands Partnership to Reduce Substance Abuse, July 28, 1993, from 12:00 to 2:00 p.m., in Rooms 11 and 12, Superior Court, Barnstable, Massachusetts.

7. The War the Police Didn't Declare and Can't Win

Joseph D. McNamara

I became a New York City policeman in 1956 and quickly became acquainted with problems of illegal drug use. I was assigned to Harlem. During the late 1950s, we cops watched in frustration as an epidemic of heroin addiction swept a community where limited opportunities created a fertile climate for escaping reality through drugs. Heroin took an awesome toll. Whole families and neighborhoods seemed to fall to addiction. Street corners were filled with young men and women nodding on their feet like zombies. Under the influence of the powerful opiate, they abruptly jerked awake, alert for a few minutes before they again drifted off. Sometimes we responded to reports of an overdose and found a muscular teenage boy dead with a hypodermic needle still in his arm.

One freezing winter night I saw a crowd of about 50 people milling about West 125th Street and Eighth Avenue close to the famous Apollo Theater. Suddenly, the group dashed to the next block. My partner on radio motor patrol explained, "The feds made a big seizure. There's a temporary shortage. They're all running because they saw a pusher get out of that cab." I have never forgotten the sight of human beings stampeding like cattle because they craved heroin. As a result of such experiences, cops were willing soldiers at the birth of the war on drugs, the term introduced by President Richard Nixon in 1972.

The consequences of drug use had become devastatingly clear to us. It seemed imperative that the government eradicate the plague of addiction. We did what police do. We arrested everyone in sight when we saw a drug violation, and we saw them constantly. But it did not take long to become disillusioned. Despite enormous increases in arrests, it was apparent that arrests neither cured users nor discouraged pushers. New pushers were on the street dealing before the cell doors closed on their predecessors. And the first thing addicts did when they got out of jail was shoot up. It was easy for working cops to believe that lenient judges and an inefficient correctional system were at fault. After all, we were working hard, making drug arrests. But doubts were growing within the police ranks. We complained of inadequate laws and sentences. The politicians responded.

The Consequences of Getting Tough

Governor Nelson Rockefeller, who had presidential ambitions, convinced the New York State legislature to pass laws giving life sentences to drug sellers and providing mandatory civil commitment for addicts. Civil commitment was abandoned within a few years because of its cost and ineffectiveness. To avoid life sentences, drug dealers recruited young boys who could only be charged with juvenile delinquency. The unintended consequence of the get-tough policy was to create legions of teenage career criminals. Patrick V. Murphy, the New York City police commissioner, had opposed the legislation for just this reason, but drug-war fever prevailed among the politicians. Civil commitments collapsed because addicts were penned up and little treatment was provided. Gradually, the courts began to take a dim view of indefinitely depriving people of their freedom without benefit of a criminal trial in the name of nonexistent treatment.

Unfortunately, the Rockefeller law's draconian penalties for low-level drug selling still persists in New York. Federal mandatory sentencing and many state laws are equally severe for drug offenses.

On the streets of Harlem we saw increases in violence stemming not from the use of heroin but from the increasingly lucrative commerce in heroin. Most of the users dozed away their lives, incapable of violence. In fact, some analysts believed that the New York teenage fighting gangs that caused great concern during the 1950s disintegrated when gang members began to use heroin. In Harlem and other poor neighborhoods, young boys who had dropped out of school and had little chance for legitimate careers suddenly saw more money than they had dreamed of and were willing to kill rivals who threatened their new affluence.

Human misery can encourage predators. On one ambulance call we found that a man named Jimmy had been having dinner with his mother. He left the table to answer the door and within moments was dead, stabbed in the heart. During a temporary shortage he had sold fake heroin to desperate addicts. To those addicts, such behavior justified killing. Addicts sometimes killed people right in front of police officers, then meekly submitted to arrest.

Why the Police Can't Win the Drug War

Street policing is not conducive to deep thinking about policy. Our skepticism grew, but we went about our job. One day, my partner and I came across a drug user. Addicts frequently used top-floor landings in apartment buildings as "shooting galleries." They would use a candle to heat water and a "nickel" bag of heroin in a bottle cap. (In those pre-inflation days, a glassine envelope containing enough heroin for a fix cost five dollars, a "nickel.") The drug users would then siphon the mixture into a spike—a makeshift syringe composed of an eyedropper and a needle. They then injected the mix into a vein swollen by the tight strip of elastic wound around their arms, legs, or wherever they could find a usable vein. Frequently, they shared needles, and as a result suffered from hepatitis B, syphilis, and other diseases. Even before the discovery of AIDS, cops dreaded accidentally pricking themselves with a needle when searching a prisoner. It might be a death sentence.

The United States Supreme Court has ruled that being an addict or having an illegal substance in your blood was not a crime,[1] but residue in the bottle cap constituted possession of an illegal substance and called for a six-months jail term, as did possession of a spike. The police lab always confirmed that the bottle cap contained a faint residue of heroin. So we drug warriors racked up another "drug arrest," although the milky stain in the bottle cap was no longer usable for injection. Drug arrest statistics serve the same purpose enemy body counts served during the Vietnam War. They are equally dubious in justifying claims of progress or victory.

One day in Harlem, the addict we arrested was cooperative. He surrendered the needle hidden in his belt, where it would be difficult to find. He pleaded with us. He was just a junkie. He couldn't take a bust right now. If we let him go he would give us a pusher. He would make a drug buy and when he and the pusher went into a hallway to exchange money for drugs we would arrest the pusher in the act and let the addict go. To my surprise, my partner agreed.

[1]Robinson v. California, 370 U.S. 660 (1962).

Since he was senior, I reluctantly went along. We put the bottle cap and needle in the glove compartment of our police car and followed the addict. It was a warm summer day and there were lots of people on Lenox Avenue as we coasted along, never more than 10 feet from our prisoner. I had my hand on the door handle ready to bolt after him if he decided to break the agreement. But he was good to his word. He walked down the street talking to one person after another. The third dealer agreed to sell. When they went into a hall-way we charged in and arrested the dealer. The addict "escaped."

What was amazing was that in bright daylight the man had talked to pushers about buying illegal drugs with a marked police car and two uniformed policemen 10 feet away. None of the men had been deterred by our presence. The first two dealers weren't being care-ful, they had already sold their supply. They had no reason to be afraid. If we had not known what the addict was doing, we might have guessed they were talking about cars, girlfriends, sports, poli-tics, or other innocent things.

For the first time, I realized how truly ineffective the police are in preventing drug use through enforcement of criminal statutes. Un-like traditional malum-in-se crimes (wrong in themselves) where a victim who is robbed or assaulted comes to the police and the crimi-nal justice system for redress and protection, drug dealing and drug use are confidential, consensual transactions between people who treasure their privacy. Every day, hundreds of thousands, perhaps millions of drug crimes occur and the police have no way of know-ing about them, let alone the ability to prevent them. The potential of being arrested and punished for a drug crime is far less than in other crimes and is not a credible deterrent to the millions of users of illegal drugs in America. And truly hard-core drug users discount the threat of arrest in proportion to their need for drugs.

The Costs of Trying to Do What Cannot Be Done

In 1972, when President Nixon called for a war against drugs, the federal drug war budget was roughly $101 million. The federal budget for the drug war in the first year of the new millennium is $17.8 billion.[2] Such numbers are difficult to comprehend, but the magnitude of the increase can be better understood if we consider that in 1972 the average monthly Social Security retirement check

[2]Office of National Drug Control Policy, 1999 Drug Strategy.

was $177, rising to approximately $900 in 1999.[3] If social security benefits had increased at the same rate as drug war spending, monthly benefits would now be $30,444. The average 1972 salary of $114 per week would have soared to $19,608 a week. If your monthly rent or mortgage payment in 1972 was $408, the same housing would now cost you $68,800 a month.

So it is fair to ask what we got for our money.

President Bill Clinton assures us we are winning the war against drugs, as did his predecessors. Yet people in law enforcement and local communities are unconvinced, and for good reason. Although it appears that casual illegal drug use has declined in recent years, regular use has not. The decline in casual drug use may be unrelated to the war on drugs, and more young people are using drugs and starting to use them at an earlier age.

Cigarette smoking and consumption of hard liquor and high-cholesterol food—all as dangerous as illegal drug use—declined because of greater awareness of health dangers, aided by truthful educational campaigns. They did not decline because consumers were jailed or because the government suppressed the supply of these substances.

During the past decade, opium production more than doubled in Southeast Asia and cocaine production grew by a third in Central and South America. Eighty to 90 percent of illegal drugs shipped to the country arrives undetected.[4] The United States, indeed the world, is awash in illegal drugs.

The vast profits resulting from prohibition—with markups as great as 17,000 percent—have led to worldwide corruption of public officials and widespread violence among drug traffickers and dealers that endangers whole nations. The United Nations reports that there is a $500 billion international black market in drugs. In the United States, drug-related overdose deaths and emergency room visits have increased. Half all high-school seniors surveyed report using an illegal drug,[5] and 85 percent of them say illegal drugs are easier to obtain than beer.[6] This, despite the fact that we have 1.8

[3]*U.S. Social Security Reports*, 1973, 1998.

[4]*Drug Policy Perspectives*, ONDCP, March 1999.

[5]*National Survey Results from Monitoring the Future Study*, Vol 1, U.S. Government Printing Office (1996).

[6]*National Survey of American Attitudes on Substance Abuse II Teens and Their Parents*, National Center for Addiction and Substance Abuse at Columbia University (1996).

million Americans behind bars and another 4 to 5 million under parole or probation. Roughly 400,000 are imprisoned for drug crimes,[7] and the illegality of drugs is related to the criminal careers of many other inmates.

Origins of the Drug War

We should understand that America's drug war started roughly 100 years ago. Protestant missionaries in China and other religious groups joined with temperance organizations to convince Congress that drugs were evil and that drug users were dangerous, immoral people. On December 17, 1914, the religious lobbyists got their version of sin outlawed in the Harrison Act. Until this federal law took effect, the nation had viewed drug use as a social and medical problem. Making possession of certain chemicals a federal crime was a radical change in policy.[8] It did not solve the drug problem but it did give birth to unanticipated social damage. It is unlikely that the Congress in 1914 would have passed the Harrison Act if it had envisioned the gigantic federal and state law enforcement, prison, and treatment bureaucracies taxpayers carry on their backs today. Ironically, those calling attention to the negative results of the unprecedented assumption of power by the federal government in 1914, and calling for drug policy reform are denounced as radical "legalizers."

I was a policeman for 35 years. As a beat officer in Harlem and as police chief in Kansas City and San Jose, I caused many drug users to be locked up. But I have come to believe that jailing people because they put chemicals into their bloodstream is a gross misuse of the police power and criminal law. Jailing drug users does not lessen drug use. Incarceration usually destroys the person's life and does immense harm to their families and neighborhoods. Justifying jail sentences by claiming that users would likely commit other crimes if they remained free is a flagrant rejection of a fundamental American right, the presumption of innocence.

[7]*Prison and Jail Inmates at Midyear 1998*, Darrell K. Gillard, Bureau Justice Statistics Bulletin, March 1999.

[8]*Organizational Decision Making and Public Policy: An Analysis of Police Drug Enforcement Strategies*, Joseph D. McNamara, doctoral dissertation, John F. Kennedy School of Government, Harvard University, 1973.

Racial Disparities

Low-income Americans and non-whites have borne the brunt of the punishment for drug offenses even though most drug use is by whites. Alfred Blumstein, former president of the American Society of Criminologists, called the drug war "an assault on the African-American community."[9] Current protests over racial profiling by the police reflect the damage that an ill-conceived war against drugs has had on the ability of local police to win the cooperation that they need to do their job.

Under the Fourth Amendment, the police, with few exceptions, are not allowed to search people or enter their homes without a warrant. Yet, last year, state and local police in the United States made approximately 1,400,000 arrests for illegal possession of drugs.[10] Overwhelmingly, these were minor arrests and rarely involved a court-approved warrant.

The inescapable conclusion is that in hundreds of thousands of cases, police officers violated their oath to uphold the Constitution and often committed perjury so that the evidence would be admitted. The practice is so prevalent that the term "testilying" is often substituted in police jargon for "testifying." The injury that unlawful searches and perjury by the police does to the credibility of our justice system is immeasurable.

Just as damaging is the destruction of trust that follows exposure of gangster cops who have robbed drug dealers, sold drugs, and framed people in the communities that they swore to protect. Police perjurers by far outnumber those cops who are predatory drug criminals; still, there have been thousands of drug-related police crimes since the 1972 declaration of a drug war.

Reform

So far, the nation has been unable to face the failure of its drug policies or to examine alternatives that would truly lessen dangerous drug use. We remain captive to myths about drug use and false stereotypes of users created a century ago by religious zealots. All drugs, including aspirin, present an element of danger to users and

---

[9]*The Search for Rationality,* paper presented as President of the American Society of Criminology, 1995.

[10]*Uniform Crime Reports, Preliminary Crime Statistics,* Federal Bureau of Investigation, 1999.

deserve caution. But in a free society, adults should be considered capable of making informed decisions about their own lives and health without the need to fear imprisonment by the government if they make unpopular or even unwise choices.

The new millennium provides the opportunity for reflection and change. Marijuana should be decriminalized. There is no record of anyone dying from marijuana or committing a murder under its effects. Any number of scientific studies have indicated that in some cases it may be an effective medicine. We would eliminate almost 700,000 arrests a year, which would save money and ruin fewer lives.

Our country should revert to the pre–Harrison Act principle that no one should be arrested if their only crime is putting certain chemicals into their bloodstream. As to "harder" drugs, we should reject the inane demagogic slogan "a drug-free America," and accept the reality that drugs will never be eradicated from our society. Drug users should be dealt with justly and humanely, if and when their use becomes a problem. But if society feels compelled to intervene in individual choices such as drug use, voluntary treatment should be substituted for arrests.

Once we are beyond the emotional straightjacket imposed long ago by the Harrison Act lobbyists, we can study how other countries minimize the harm caused by drugs. The Swiss, for example, found during a five-year experiment that providing heroin to addicts actually reduced heroin use and significantly reduced the crime committed by the addicts. The Netherlands regulates and controls the distribution of small amounts of hashish and marijuana and has a lower per capita use of drugs, and lower crime rates than the United States.

There is no panacea, but it is clear that doggedly continuing a policy that has failed for nearly a century is no way to start a new century. Why is it that in the land of the free and the home of the brave, individual freedom of choice is so terrifying that we are willing to incarcerate, often under barbarous conditions, people whose only crime is an unconventional lifestyle?

8. Call Off the Hounds

David Klinger

Since stepping down as a sworn law enforcement officer some 15 years ago after brief stints as a street cop in Los Angeles and then Redmond, Washington, I have not devoted much professional attention to the problem of illicit drugs. I pursued and obtained advanced degrees in the social sciences, joined the faculty of a large state university, pursued a research agenda, secured tenure, and, recently, took another academic job at another large university. While teaching, my dealings with drugs have been tangential—a few lectures about drug abuse in a course on the sociology of deviance, a week devoted to the drug/crime nexus in a criminology course.

The subject of illicit drugs has played an even smaller role in the service component of my academic life. In training I provide for domestic violence counselors, lectures I offer to police officers, and interviews I give to the press, the drug issue nearly always stays far in the background. Over the years, the drug issue has played an equally small role in my research, the major focus of which is sorting out how various factors affect the actions of street police officers during their interactions with citizens. A recent shift in my research gaze, however, has led me to direct more attention to the topic of drugs.

For reasons that have nothing to do with drug enforcement, I became increasingly interested in the organization and operations of police special weapons and tactics (SWAT) teams. Because SWAT teams in many places around our nation are heavily involved in enforcing drug laws, primarily by serving warrants authorizing police officers to search specific locations for illegal drugs, and because their actions in some cases have drawn criticism, many colleagues, students, officers I know and help train, and members of the fourth estate have sought my opinion about various aspects of current drug policy. Such inquiries have led me to articulate positions on a number of issues, some which I have held for years, and others that have formed only recently as I was compelled to consider them for the first time.

The issue I am asked about most often is the current strategy of pursuing a "war on drugs" through our legal system to remove illicit intoxicants from our nation. After several times trying to give nuanced answers by addressing specific sub-issues and seeing that I was boring my listeners, I changed my approach to the question and began to say simply, "I think we should legalize 'em." Most people do not expect to hear such words from an ex-street cop who spends a lot of time with SWAT teams. My answer typically leads to surprise, followed by an engaging discussion about why I believe that the use of currently forbidden drugs should be legalized and what we should do instead of pursuing a policy of blanket prohibition.

Contemplating Drugs

When I joined the LAPD in late 1980, I was a strong supporter of the notion that drugs that were illegal should remain illegal, and that the enforcement of drug laws should be a top priority for all police officers and agencies. I went to high school in an area of Southern California notable for its association with illegal drugs. Much of the marijuana and other drugs coming out of Mexico in the mid-1970s was off-loaded nearby from a variety of border-crossing conveyances and prepared for distribution throughout the nation. Moreover, many of my classmates were known to ingest copious quantities of drugs such as pot, speed, and Quaaludes. During my daily stroll to school I often smelled the sweet stench that wafted from the reefer some of the bolder students smoked while standing just outside the fence at the edge of the campus. During my high school years, I saw firsthand the havoc that such behavior caused in the lives of those who partook, as well as the disruption it caused the community, and figured that busting anyone and everyone associated with illegal drugs was the way to make things better.

My belief that thorough enforcement of tough laws was the way to go grew during my college years as I prepared for a career in police work. But it diminished rapidly after I graduated from the LAPD academy and hit the streets. Assigned to the rugged 77th

Street Division in the heart of South Central Los Angeles, I saw a surfeit of illegal drugs and observed the social problems that one could find in any community awash in the trafficking and use of marijuana, cocaine, heroin, PCP, and the other controlled substances that were widely available in America in the early 1980s. At some point in my first months on patrol, after handling hundreds of calls that involved drugs, and after arresting scores of people for possessing various sorts of illegal stuff, I began to have doubts about what my peers and I were doing. I saw violent criminals walking the streets because the jail space they rightfully deserved was occupied by nonviolent drug offenders. When we carted small-time drug dealers off to the hoosegow, I saw other sellers quickly step in to fill the void. I started seeing most of the people I dealt with who had some association with drugs either as broken souls who made self-destructive choices or harmless people who indulged their appetites in moderation—but not as crooks who needed to be punished. And except for the odd encounter with whacked-out individuals who had ingested more of some mind-bending drug, such as PCP, than their systems could handle, and the occasional call about someone who had overdosed on some kind of dope, I found much more misery associated with alcohol than I did with any forbidden pharmaceuticals.

I tried to reconcile what I saw with the stance I held about the need to firmly enforce the drug laws. At first I accepted the arguments of politicians, policy wonks, and my peers who asserted that ever harsher laws and firmer enforcement would turn back the tide of illegal drugs washing over our beleaguered nation. By the time I left Los Angeles for Washington state, however, I had begun my transition from drug law supporter to legalization advocate. Near the end of my tenure with the LAPD I came to believe that marijuana—a drug I had never seen anyone overdose on or influence anyone to do anything more violent than attack a bag of potato chips—should be legalized. I had dealt with a few folks who had smoked some pot, jumped behind the wheel of a car, and driven recklessly, but I came to see that driving under the influence of marijuana was not much different from driving under the influence of alcohol. Both actions involved the use of a drug in an irresponsible and dangerous manner that the law could, and should, respond to with severe sanctions. Both behaviors posed a substantial threat to people other than the reprobates who engaged in it.

The same logic did not apply to the many other illegal substances,

129

such as cocaine, heroin, PCP, and various "designer drugs" readily available from southern California to the suburbs of Seattle. These drugs were clearly causing major problems in two populations—users and the rest of us. Among users, the primary problems were the ruined lives of those who could not control their appetites and the lives lost by overdose. For the rest of us, the main problems were violent acts committed by people who were out of control while under the influence of such drugs, property crimes committed by regular users to support their habits, and violence committed by those battling it out for control of illegal drug markets. Many a citizen took some lumps (or worse) from some whacked-out idiot high on some dangerous drug, and many a cop got into knock-down, drag-out fights with such people. Many citizens lost cash or other valuables to drug users who turned to violent crime in order to indulge their illegal appetites. And many a person was killed or crippled by drug dealers whose hunger for market share motivated them to spray bullets about the streets.

Completing the Turn

I held a bifurcated stance toward illicit drugs—legalize pot but strictly enforce existing laws against the rest of the stuff—throughout my tenure with the Redmond Police Department and into my graduate studies. As the years passed, however, I saw a nation fighting harder and harder, devoting more and more money, and jailing more and more citizens who used and/or dealt drugs, all the while falling farther and farther behind in the war on drugs. The price of the drugs didn't rise in the face of increased interdiction efforts; the rate of usage wasn't falling; and the number of lives damaged or destroyed by chronic use, overdose, and associated criminal activities mounted. I became convinced that we needed to make a major change in how we dealt with illegal drugs.

I saw it as a time to either retrench or retreat, fish or cut bait. I came to believe that it was time to truly make war against drugs, or to give up the ghost. We needed to turn the rhetorical war into a real war, take the fight to the sources of the drugs, and lay waste the people and places producing and distributing them. Or else we needed to call it quits and legalize illicit drugs.

In real wars warriors die. There are few things worth dying for, and none of those things obtain in the drug war. As I pondered why America was awash in drugs, I saw that the problem lay not in the places sending us the stuff—the Colombias, Thailands, and Af-ghanistans of the world—but here in the United States, where the desires of millions of Americans created a massive demand. It made no sense to me to send Americans to die on foreign soil because some of their fellow citizens wanted to smoke, snort, and inject substances grown over there.

I thought about what our troops would be doing overseas once they got there: killing people and blowing things up, which is what militaries do in wars. I thought about who and what they would be doing it to. Most of the people killed would likely be peasants involved in the drug trade in order to eke out a living in the third-world nations where they lived. And much of what would get blown up would be things that poor people and their families and communities needed for survival. As is the case with being killed, in my mind, one should kill or otherwise ruin the lives of fellow hu-man beings for very few reasons. I do not count supplying my neighbor with something he wants as one of them. If the real source of the U.S. drug problem lay within our borders, the notion of sending U.S. troops to search out and destroy drug producers and suppliers abroad was unsettling.

The third major thing I reflected on as I contemplated the "real war" option was what would happen to our nation if we were to undertake such an effort. Despite the fact that most Americans held an antidrug stance and supported the war on drugs rhetoric, a real war against drugs would not be a popular one. It would not be short, for the scope of the problem and the nature of the terrain would necessitate a protracted military effort. It would be expen-sive, for large-scale overseas deployments are. It would bring in-creased tension between our nation and others and anger many of our allies. And as the 19-year-old volunteers started to come home in body bags, the nation would be forced to reflect on whether fighting a war to stop drugs was worth its many costs. Lack of public support would seal the fate of a military adventure and further erode our ability to engage in legitimate operations over-seas.

Thus, I rejected the military option. But even as I did, I could not bring myself to accept legalizing illicit drugs. The idea resonated poorly with the street cop inside me.

I went back over the ground I'd previously covered, but found nothing that might lead me to change my conclusion that tough laws and rigid enforcement were doomed to fail. Not only did I find nothing to change my mind about the futility of drug prohibition there, but I encountered many pieces of evidence that our drug policy was actually counterproductive in terms of making our nation a better place to live. I came to realize that many of the social problems associated with the use of illegal drugs are exacerbated, if not caused by, the fact that they are illegal.

If drugs that are currently illegal were regulated in the same manner as legal substances, the problems of unintentional overdose and injury from impurities would diminish considerably. The prohibition of drugs also increases rates of predatory crime. Because the price of illegal drugs is far higher than it would be if they were not forbidden, people who resort to crime to support drug habits commit more crimes for a given amount of drugs than they would if drugs were legally produced, distributed, and sold. A similar phenomenon drove up the homicide rates in many major cities during the late 1980s. Murders that occurred as individuals and gangs fought for control of the drug trade would not have occurred had there been no lucrative illegal market to squabble over. These unintended consequences of the failed prohibition policy helped make the case for legalization.

When I reflected on what prohibition was doing to our legal system, the first thing I noted was that it was spawning law enforcement corruption scandals across the land. Cops and other public officials who violate their oath by taking bribes and engaging in similar corrupt practices should be severely punished, for they dishonor their profession and weaken the fragile bond of trust between government and the governed that holds our republic together.

At the same time, corruption occurs in specific social contexts and thrives best when the prospective payoff is high and the risk of sanction is small, a combination that fits the drug picture to a tee. Because the illegal drug trade produces many billions of dollars in profits, there is plenty of money to tempt officers with incredible paydays for looking the other way, ripping off dealers, dealing drugs themselves, and similar unsavory actions. And because admitting involvement with illegal drugs can have legal repercussions, the victims, associates, and accomplices of corrupt cops are unlikely to turn them in. Drug scandals rocked police agency after police agency in the 1980s and '90s, from New York to Miami and all points west. With each scandal, the trust of the citizenry in police officers and agencies took another hit. In some places citizens simply assume that their cops are on the take from drug dealers or in cahoots with them. Our great nation is weakened by such cynicism and may have already suffered crippling harm from the corrosive effects of drug-related corruption. I know it made my job harder when I was a cop. Police officers are human and humans can be tempted by big, low-risk payoffs.

Perhaps first among the bedrock principles on which our nation sits—one that was drummed into me from elementary school through the police academy—is the notion that the state may sanction only those citizens whose guilt of a criminal offense it can establish beyond a reasonable doubt. When I joined the LAPD, I had never heard of the term "asset forfeiture." By the time I left law enforcement, it was a familiar term and I had become quite familiar with how it was used. Asset forfeiture refers to seizing property that is (in specific ways) associated with the use of illegal drugs. I thought to myself, "Sounds good to me; drug dealers shouldn't be able to keep stuff that they obtain illegally or use to commit their crimes." As I learned about the specifics, however, I became a skeptic. Two things caused me great concern. The first was that the agency that seized the property got to keep some or even all of it. This seemed an invitation to corruption. The second thing was that the burden of proof for seizing property under the asset forfeiture laws was unnervingly low: mere probable cause. Some well-intentioned folk decided that the threat posed by illegal drugs was so great that we needed to dispense with the usual proving beyond reasonable doubt and simply take people's property because there was probable cause to believe that they were involved in certain ways with drugs.

After leaving police work, my concerns about asset forfeiture laws grew as I watched police agencies around the nation use them more and more. I saw agency after agency finance more and more programs with seized assets. I heard more and more horror stories about people losing their homes, cars, and cash to a state that could never have proven beyond a reasonable doubt that the suspects had any involvement in the use of, much less the trade in, illegal drugs. I could no longer hold my nose in the face of such rotten abuses and decided that the asset forfeiture laws should be scrapped, that our nation needed to return to the core principle that the state can seize the property of citizens suspected of involvement in criminal activity only when and if it can prove involvement beyond a reasonable doubt.

I conducted a concerted search for reasons why we should maintain prohibition, found only evidence against the idea, and reached the conclusion that no matter how much I didn't like the idea, our nation should change course and legalize currently illicit drugs.

Will Legalization Work?

During the several years since I first reached the conclusion that we should call off the hounds, I have discussed my ideas with people in many walks of life. Interestingly, both my hardiest supporters and my harshest critics come from the same group: my law enforcement associates. Many of them—on both sides of the debate—share my views about the futility of the drug war and agree that it brings with it a substantial downside. What generally separates those who agree with me from those who don't is their take on a question that they almost invariably put to me: Won't legalizing drugs lead more people to take them, and thus make things worse?

My answer to their double-barreled question is two-fold. I answer the second part of it first by asserting that even if more people do take drugs in the wake of legalization, we would live in a society where citizens suffer far less from the predatory crimes spawned by the illicit drug trade and would not have to worry that state agents might seize their property with no compelling evidence of guilt. I do not know whether legalizing drugs that are currently illegal will increase their popularity, but I suspect that if we approach legalization thoughtfully and pursue a sensible post-legalization strategy, then the drug rolls will not swell; they may in fact decline.

The approach I have in mind consists first of an honest scientific assessment of the dangers of specific drugs. What do they do in the short term to one's mind and body? What effects do they have in the long term? How easy is it for one to become dependent on them? The second aspect in the pre-legalization process would be to disseminate the findings widely so that the American people have reliable facts about specific substances. The third component would involve people telling their state and federal governments (through hearings, petitions, and the like) their feelings on the relative dangers of various drugs to determine what warnings public officials and government agencies should disseminate to inform people about each specific drug about to be legalized. The fourth aspect of my plan would involve a concerted effort by community groups, educators, religious and civic leaders, and the public at large to forcefully speak out against the use of those drugs that are truly dangerous. The people may well determine that some of the currently illegal drugs are not dangerous and therefore that they will not be part of the antidrug campaign. Once legalization arrives, the antidrug campaign would continue and even expand.

This framework of education and condemnation rests on the well-established principle that most of the people most of the time will follow the rules when the norms are clearly articulated, the reasons for them are made apparent, and violations are met with open disapproval. Even though we live in a society that has erected a massive latticework of laws to regulate conduct, the primary reason most of us conform has little to do with the law and much to do with pleasing others. In other words, more than fear of the law, we are governed by potent systems of informal social control. We have forgotten this in the battle against dangerous drugs. It is time to recover this memory and return to informal means of social control.

We cannot protect free adults from their own poor choices, and we should not use the force of law to try. If my research and education plan were instituted, we would spend substantial time and resources urging individuals to make wise choices. In a free society negative consequences befall people who use their freedom to do foolish things. Victimless, self-destructive behavior is its own punishment, not the business of the legal system.

The regime of legalization I envision would include control of the drug trade by state governments. Drugs would be produced by the states or under their license with strict adherence to purity and dosing standards, and sold to adults in state-run stores similar to those that sell liquor in many states. That way, there will be fewer bad reactions to drug ingestion than is currently the case.

Of course, there should be strict laws strictly enforced against dangerous behavior such as driving while under the influence of drugs. This component of legalization would be similar to the current state of affairs regarding the use of public space while intoxicated. And I would argue for a true zero-tolerance policy for such activity, with long stretches of incarceration for those who get high and endanger others. If the rest of us are going to accede to the desires of those who wish to take dangerous substances, then those who endanger others should be punished severely. In a similar vein, anyone who commits a crime of violence while under the influence would be punished severely. Indeed, no longer would the law view intoxication a mitigating factor. Rather, intoxication would increase the punishment of those convicted of violent crime.

Those who would supply to juveniles substances deemed dangerous should likewise suffer severe punishment. The program I propose is predicated on a framework of adults freely making informed choices, but paying the price for making poor ones.

I am not calling for our nation to throw in the towel in the struggle against dangerous drugs. Rather, I am calling for a shift in strategy from using the blunt instrument of criminal law as our primary weapon to using the subtle tools of education, national condemnation, community pressure, family shaming, individual rebuke, and the like as our key means to try to prevent people from indulging in dangerous drugs and to get users to stop. The criminal law would still be a crucial instrument in the process, but moved to the periphery, where it can be used against those whose behavior harms others, not just themselves. Call the hounds off the poor fools who choose to take harmful drugs and sic them on drug users who present a direct danger to people besides themselves.

The Role of SWAT Teams in Our Current Antidrug Strategy

Some people have expressed concern about the use of SWAT teams to execute warrants signed by judges authorizing police to search specific locations for illegal drugs. The core of the argument put forth by those opposed to the use of SWAT teams for serving narcotics warrants is that SWAT teams—with their "military" equipment, organization, training, and tactics—act more like soldiers than police officers and thus are more likely to use unnecessary force against citizens than would be the case if the warrants were served by non-SWAT officers. This argument betrays a lack of understanding of how SWAT officers are equipped and organized, what they do when serving narcotics warrants, why they are equipped and organized the way they are, and why they do what they do. A thorough discussion of these issues would take more space than is appropriate in this forum, so I will simply provide an overview and invite any interested readers to contact me if they wish additional information.

People need to understand that serving narcotics warrants is dangerous business. We know that many people in the narcotics trade keep firearms and other dangerous weapons handy in order to protect themselves, their stash, and their cash from competitors, thieves, and the police. Many a cop has confronted persons brandishing weapons inside warrant locations, and many a cop has been shot at or shot while serving narcotics warrants. When cops see people pointing guns at them they tend to shoot, and when they get shot at, they tend to shoot back. Over the years, consequently, the business of serving narcotics warrants has included a goodly amount of gunfire between the cops and people at locations being searched and, ipso facto, a goodly number of injuries and deaths.

The primary mission of SWAT teams is to save lives. Thus, the organization of teams, the weapons and other accouterments they wear and carry, the training they do, and the tactics they employ are all designed to reduce the likelihood that anyone—cop, suspect, and innocent citizen alike—will be fatally harmed in any of the various high-risk jobs they are called upon to handle. If push comes to shove, of course, SWAT cops will use deadly force to prevent serious or life-threatening harm to themselves or other innocent parties. But experience has proven time and again that well-armed, well-trained, well-organized, and well-outfitted cops who employ proper tactics can peaceably resolve many situations that might otherwise result in gunplay. Experience shows that when cops do find themselves in situations where deadly force is necessary, fewer people are injured when properly equipped, well-trained cops handle matters.

The number of shootings during the service of narcotics warrants grew during the '80s and '90s. Police departments around the nation determined that one way to reduce the number of shootings, and thus the number of people injured during drug raids, was to use their best-armed, best-trained, best-organized, best-outfitted, and most tactically sound officers—i.e., their SWAT teams—to serve at least some narcotics warrants. Thus, as a means to reduce the number of police shootings and the resultant deaths or injuries, SWAT teams got involved in serving narcotics warrants in a big way.

Overall, the use of SWAT teams to serve narcotics warrants accomplished what it was intended to do. In case after case the use of SWAT cops to serve narcotics warrants has saved the lives of suspects who almost surely would have been shot by regular officers. And in numerous cases the only reason cops serving narcotics warrants took no casualties was the fact that they were experienced SWAT officers who were able to call upon their specialized experience and resources to save their lives. On the flip side of the coin, some citizens and officers have been shot in circumstances where they would not have been injured or killed had a sound SWAT team served the warrant.

137

Because the evidence indicates that the use of SWAT teams to serve narcotics warrants leads to lower levels of violence between citizens and the police, I believe that SWAT teams play an important role within the framework of our current prohibitionist policy toward dangerous drugs. While I oppose the war on drugs, until we call off the hounds, we should use SWAT teams to help fight it. We owe it to the citizens who place their lives in danger by breaking our unwise laws and, especially, to the cops who daily risk their lives implementing our failed policies.

PART IV

THE POLITICAL AND SOCIAL EFFECTS
OF THE DRUG WAR

9. Effects of the Drug War

Julie Stewart

Ten years ago I worked as director of public affairs for the Cato Institute. I had no idea then that I would one day become an expert on sentencing, but life has a way of throwing you curve balls. The curve ball I received was the sentencing and incarceration of my only brother, Jeff, in 1990 for growing marijuana.

His case is not the worst I have seen, nor is it the best. But at the time, it was the only one I knew about. Even today it still illustrates what is wrong with the mandatory minimum sentencing laws that I have spent the past nine years trying to overturn.

Jeff was leading a relatively unproductive life in Washington state. He was 35 years old and he was smoking marijuana every day when he and two friends decided they could grow their own pot, have a ready supply, and sell some of it to their friends. They set up a grow-room in a garage on property that Jeff owned and on which his two friends lived. They filled the room with as many little pots as would fit (about 365) and started their seedlings.

When the plants were about 5–6 inches tall, the friends who lived on the property invited the neighbor over to smoke a joint and then showed him the grow-room. The neighbor subsequently called the police and received a $1,000 reward for turning in the pot-growers. When the two men were arrested, they quickly gave up my brother's name in exchange for a reduction in sentence. The system worked beautifully.

Both of the men had prior felony convictions for drug offenses, and one of them had served time in a California prison for a drug offense. But in exchange for informing on my brother, they both got probation. If they had not provided "substantial assistance" to the prosecutor, they would have received the same sentence that Jeff did (or perhaps more, due to their priors). Instead, Jeff ended up holding the bag and received a federal prison sentence of five years, without parole. When Jeff was arrested, I was at Cato working. I

141

vividly remember his phone call from jail to my office. When he told me that he had been arrested for growing marijuana, my first thought was "how stupid of you"; my second thought was "well, it's *only* marijuana." Little did I know that there is no such thing as "only" marijuana anymore.

Jeff ended up pleading guilty because the prosecutor threatened him with a 15-year sentence if he took his case to trial. This is a common tactic—they charge you with every possible offense, then offer to drop some of them if you agree to plead guilty. The statistics show that the government wins in 96 percent of the cases that go to trial. Even for the innocent, the risk is very high. Jeff was not innocent and knew he would lose at trial, so he pleaded guilty. In exchange, he was given a "mere" five years in prison, instead of the possible 15 years.

At Jeff's sentencing, his judge, Judge Robert McNichols from the Eastern District of Washington (who is now deceased) made a strong statement opposing the sentence he was forced by law to impose on Jeff. He described being a senior district court judge who had been on the bench for 25 years, yet deemed unfit by act of Congress to determine the appropriate sentence in my brother's case. Instead, a young federal prosecutor straight out of law school was empowered to tell him what sentence he must deliver.

Those were the comments that motivated me to leave the Cato Institute and start a nonprofit organization to change mandatory minimum sentencing laws. What kind of a justice system was it where the judge no longer had sentencing power? And why was Jeff prosecuted federally in the first place—he had not crossed state lines; it was not a DEA bust. All of this was completely contrary to everything I had learned about our criminal justice system in school. I was outraged that American voters had allowed this to happen and that nothing was being done to stop it.

I've learned a lot in the past nine years. The first thing I learned is that mandatory minimum sentencing laws are not new—they've been around for over 200 years. In 1991, the U.S. Sentencing Commission published a report on mandatory minimum sentences at the request of Congress.[1] The report lists all of the mandatory minimum sentencing laws on the books, starting in 1790 when piracy on the high seas resulted in a prison sentence of life without parole.

---

[1]*Special Report to Congress: Mandatory Minimum Penalties in the Federal Criminal Justice System*, U.S. Sentencing Commission, August 1991.

There are more than 100 separate federal mandatory minimum penalty provisions located in 60 different criminal statutes. They make for a fascinating historical tour of the crime du jour:

- In 1857, refusal to testify before Congress resulted in a sentence of one month in prison;
- In 1887, securities violations relating to transfer or issuance was a one-year prison sentence;
- In 1888, bribery of an inspector of Baltimore or New York harbors resulted in a six-month prison sentence;
- In 1888, refusal to operate railroad or telegraph lines brought a six-month sentence;
- In 1915, the unauthorized practice of pharmacy resulted in a one-month sentence;
- In 1948, treason and sedition was five years in prison;
- In 1965, first degree murder of a U.S. president or member of his staff was life in prison;
- In 1974, skyjacking resulted in 20 years in prison.[2]

So you can see how historically (and perhaps hysterically) Congress has responded to what it perceives the current major national threat, passing a mandatory prison sentence for it. But in the mid-1980s, Congress outdid itself. Between 1984 and 1990 members of Congress enacted four statutes that account for 94 percent of the cases sentenced under mandatory minimums. Those four statutes are for drug and gun offenses.

The laws were enacted with haste, without the benefit of hearings or any analysis of their likely impact. Grossly overcrowded prisons and race-based disparities in punishment have resulted. The new legislation was driven by another "crime du jour"—the cocaine overdose of University of Maryland basketball star Len Bias, and by the rise of crack cocaine. Congress passed laws sentencing defendants with a specific quantity of drugs to mandatory prison sentences of predetermined length, generally five or ten years without parole. No mitigating factors could be considered, and only the prosecutor would have the discretion to reduce the sentence based on his or her subjective determination that "substantial assistance" had been provided—that the accused had turned in others ripe for prosecution.

[2]Ibid. Appendix A, pages A1 through A8.

The impact of these laws has been stunning. Not in any reduction of drug use, but in the denial of liberty to thousands of nonviolent drug offenders who now crowd our prisons. In 1986, when the majority of the drug mandatory minimums were passed, 38 percent of the federal prison population were drug offenders. Today, that number is 60 percent.[3] In 1998, 57 percent of drug defendants entering federal prison were first offenders, and 88 percent of them had no weapons.[4]

We are not catching drug kingpins. We are catching the little guys, the girlfriends, the mules, and we are sending them to prison for 5 years, 10 years, and often much longer. And politicians largely don't give a damn. They don't care that we are destroying the lives of these defendants, labeling them forever "felons," removing them from their families, often leaving wives and children without a breadwinner.

There are more than 133,000 people in federal prison today, and 80,000 of them are there for drug offenses. Their average sentence is 76 months—nearly 6.5 years behind bars. They are people like my brother, and Denese Calixte, a 51-year-old mother of seven when she was convicted of possession with intent to distribute crack cocaine and sentenced to 10 years in prison. Her offense? After falling from a ladder while picking fruit in Florida to support her family, Denese injured her neck and could no longer work. A man who sold small quantities of drugs in her neighborhood asked Denese if he could occasionally leave his drugs with her overnight, for which he would pay her $200 each night. The drugs were stored in a pill bottle or cigar tube (not exactly a kingpin quantity). Somehow the police found out and broke into Denese's house and found the drugs. She is still in prison.

Linda Lee Messer, who as a 45-year-old mother of three working as a housekeeper earning $6.50 an hour, was sentenced to five years in prison for manufacturing marijuana. The sheriff's department received a tip that there was marijuana growing on property belonging to Linda and her husband. When they searched the property, they found 184 seedlings and 1,000 grams of processed marijuana. The case was referred to the U.S. District Court and the jury deadlocked in Linda's first trial. She was found guilty in the second trial. At sentencing, Judge William Stafford of the U.S. District

[3]Federal Bureau of Prisons, "Quickfacts," December 1998.
[4]U.S. Sentencing Commission Sourcebook, 1998, pp. 72–74.

144

Court, Northern District of Florida, said: "These local matters, it seems to me, are dealt with better on a local level, or else the federal court becomes so trivialized that it no longer has room for the real important national cases."

Todd Davidson, who was 21 years old and following the Grateful Dead on tour when he was arrested in Florida for conspiracy to possess with intent to distribute LSD, was sent to federal prison. The circumstances surrounding his arrest and incarceration were remarkable. He and a fellow "Deadhead" were sharing a motel room where the fellow Deadhead had arranged for several LSD deals with undercover agents. When they busted him, Todd was arrested as well, even though he never participated in any of the deals. He is serving a 10-year sentence.

These are the "dangerous drug offenders" now filling America's federal prisons; they are just a few of the 400,000 drug defendants serving state and federal prison sentences across the land.

This is a shameful period in American history. I look forward to the day that we, as a nation, look back on this period with horror— wondering how we could have incarcerated so many nonviolent offenders for so many years.

We must repeal these mandatory minimum sentencing laws. That will not be drug-law reform, but it will be life-saving. There are changes we can make today, that will immediately make a difference in the lives of people already sentenced, or those who will soon be sentenced.

Last year in Michigan, FAMM succeeded in getting Michigan's heinous drug-lifer law changed to allow for parole after 15 years. It is an incremental change, but it meant immediate freedom for four nonviolent drug prisoners serving life sentences, and the possibility of freedom for 200 others.

In Congress, Rep. Maxine Waters (D-CA), has introduced legislation to repeal the mandatory minimum sentencing laws for drug offenders. Waters may not be some people's first choice for carrying the torch of sentencing reform, but she is the only member of Congress with the guts to do it, and we applaud her for it. More lawmakers need to take a stand for justice for the thousands of nonviolent drug offenders who are rotting in America's prisons.

10. Collateral Damage: The Wide-Ranging Consequences of America's Drug War

Ted Galen Carpenter

President Richard M. Nixon declared "war" on illegal drugs nearly three decades ago. In 1986, President Ronald Reagan gave substance to that metaphor by issuing a presidential directive that drug trafficking constituted a national security threat. Reagan's directive authorized the U.S. military and U.S. intelligence agencies to become involved in the effort to prevent illegal drugs from entering the United States. Advocates of the prohibitionist strategy routinely refer to drug use, no matter how casual or infrequent, as posing a threat to America's safety and well-being akin to the armed threat posed by enemy states or terrorist movements. Given that mindset, it is perhaps appropriate that the White House Office of National Drug Control Policy is directed by a general (albeit a retired one), Barry McCaffrey.

It is tempting to sneer at the drug warriors' rhetorical overkill, but that would be a mistake. The war mentality is by no means confined to rhetoric and titles. The tactics resorted to are evidence that the term "war" is no longer just a metaphor.[1]

As in any war, there is an ever-growing roster of innocent victims: people who have the bad fortune to run afoul of warriors pursuing their objective with crushing intensity, sometimes people simply in the wrong place at the wrong time. War inevitably produces undesirable (usually unintended) side effects. War is bad for the health of

---

[1]The war on drugs even includes a full-blown propaganda campaign featuring a $195 million media blitz on the evils of drug use. The government's anti-drug advertising campaign is larger than the campaigns of such companies as American Express, Nike, and Sprint. Roberto Suro, "Government Blankets Media With Anti-Drug Message for Youth," *Washington Post*, July 9, 1998, p. A9.

civil liberties—everyone's civil liberties. The history of America's armed conflicts demonstrates the truth of that observation. During the War between the States, President Abraham Lincoln illegally suspended of the writ of habeas corpus, allowed the trial of civilians before military tribunals, and countenanced many other abuses.

Upon America's entry into World War I, the administration of Woodrow Wilson imposed pervasive censorship, jailed pacifists and other opponents of the war, and presided over a veritable reign of terror against German-Americans. During World War II, President Franklin Roosevelt ordered the detention of Japanese-Americans in "relocation centers"—a euphemism for concentration camps. The Vietnam War saw the military, Central Intelligence Agency, and Federal Bureau of Investigation conduct illegal surveillance of antiwar groups while attempting to discredit them through disinformation campaigns.[2] The historical record should give pause to Americans who believe that it is proper for the U.S. government to wage a war against a domestic enemy, U.S. citizens who opt to use unapproved mind-altering substances.

Only an incurable optimist would argue that America's 30-year war against drugs has been a success. Although the percentage of Americans using illegal drugs is down from the peak levels of the late 1970s and early 1980s, use is still widespread and, indeed, is significantly higher than it was when Nixon issued his declaration of war. Despite the expenditure of more than $300 billion dollars by federal, state, and local governments over those three decades (the federal government alone spent $16 billion in 1998) on efforts to stem the trade, drugs remain cheap and easily available throughout the United States. Prices of cocaine and other drugs have generally shown a downward trend—a reliable indicator of a plentiful supply.[3]

The original Thirty Years' War, which brought much misery to the people of Central Europe, finally ended with the Treaty of Westphalia in 1648. Unfortunately, no comparable end to the current thirty-years war is in sight. (Perhaps the drug warriors wish to

---

[2]For a discussion of the destructive effect of wartime policies on the First Amendment and other constitutional protections of civil liberties, see Ted Galen Carpenter, *The Captive Press: Foreign Policy Crises and the First Amendment* (Washington: Cato Institute, 1995), pp. 13–44; 107–119; 125–131; 141–150.

[3]Glenn Frankel, "U.S. War on Drugs Yields Few Victories," *Washington Post,* June 8, 1997. p. A1.

replicate the Hundred Years' War between England and France.) As is so often the case with failing wars, fanatical proponents prefer escalation to surrender or compromise. It is indicative of such a mentality that advocates of the drug war seek additional increases in an already bloated budget and wage campaigns of vilification against such modest proposals as legalizing the limited medical use of marijuana.

Calls to escalate the war on drugs must be firmly rebuffed. The current drug war has already caused major social disruptions, both in the United States and several drug-producing countries in Latin America, and has badly eroded important liberties guaranteed by the U.S. Constitution.[4] An escalation could cause social and political havoc in portions of the Western Hemisphere and pose a mortal threat to the remaining civil liberties of Americans—even Americans far removed from the drug issue.

Some Prominent Examples of Collateral Damage

Critics of the war on drugs have documented numerous disastrous side-effects of the prohibitionist strategy.[5] They have pointed out that more than 60 percent of the inmates in federal prisons and 25 percent of the inmates in state prisons are incarcerated for drug offenses. The explosion in the size of prison populations (increases of 160 percent at the federal level and 126 percent at the state level between the mid-1980s and mid-1990s alone)[6] has not only caused overcrowding but has led to the early release of prisoners—including individuals convicted of violent crimes—to make cells available for drug offenders. Books and studies by antiprohibitionists have also shown how the drug war led to violent struggles between rival gangs over control of the black market in American cities, spawning a spiraling crime rate during the 1980s

[4]Peter Andreas aptly describes these tendencies as signaling the rise of the "crimefare state," which has supplanted the Cold War era specter of a "national security state." Peter Andreas, "The Rise of the American Crimefare State," *World Policy Journal* (Fall 1997): 38–45.

[5]For a good overview, see Steven Wisotsky, *Beyond the War on Drugs: Overcoming a Failed Public Policy* (Buffalo, N.Y.: Prometheus, 1990). Also see James Bovard, *Lost Rights: The Destruction of American Liberty* (New York: St. Martin's Press, 1994), pp. 199–257.

[6]Frankel.

and early 1990s until most of the turf battles were sorted out.[7] Those conflicts not only destabilized entire neighborhoods but produced a tragically long list of innocent victims caught in the crossfire. Given the economics of prohibition, such a result was inevitable—as should have been learned from a similar upsurge of violence in the 1920s when the United States government attempted to outlaw the sale of alcoholic beverages.[8]

Scholarly analyses have provided compelling evidence that the war on drugs has led to an inexorable erosion of the protections against unreasonable searches and seizures provided by the Fourth Amendment.[9] Police have far greater latitude than they did a few decades ago to search automobiles (and sometimes the occupants) following routine traffic stops. Motorists who fit the "profile" of probable drug couriers developed by law enforcement bureaucracies are especially at risk for such stops and the subsequent searches.[10]

The situation is not yet as bad with regard to searches of homes and businesses, but there are ominous trends in that direction. Search warrants are frequently issued on information provided by informants that law enforcement authorities believe credible. In a distressing number of instances, that belief proves unfounded—sometimes with tragic consequences. The preferred method of conducting raids in suspected narcotics violation cases—"no-knock," break-in-the-door searches of homes, often in the middle of the night—has compounded the danger. In August 1999, such a raid resulted in the death of a 64-year-old grandfather. He and his family were asleep in their beds when police searching for illegal drugs broke down the front door. The victim was shot in the back. Apparently believing (not unreasonably) that a break-in by criminals was underway and his family was in danger, he had reached into a

---

[7]Sam Staley, *Drug Policy and the Decline of American Cities* (New Brunswick, N.J.: Transaction, 1992).

[8]Mark Thornton, *The Economics of Prohibition* (Salt Lake City: University of Utah Press, 1991).

[9]Even some early analyses warned of the trend and noted that the war on drugs was the principal factor in the narrowing of Fourth Amendment protections. See Silas J. Wasserstrom, "The Incredible Shrinking Fourth Amendment," *American Criminal Law Review* 21, no. 3 (Winter 1984): 257–401.

[10]Advocates of the drug war defend profiling even though they admit the process snares a disproportionate number of young minority males. See Clayton Searle, "Profiling in Law Enforcement," *Washington Times*, September 9, 1999, p. A 21. Searle is the president of the International Narcotics Interdiction Association.

nightstand drawer where he kept a gun. No drugs were found anywhere on the premises.[11] Typically, the drug warriors and their defenders dismiss such episodes as tragic accidents. Unfortunately, such "accidents" are becoming all too common.[12]

The war on drugs has undermined the Fourth Amendment's protection against unreasonable seizures at least as badly as it has diluted the protection against unreasonable searches. Rep. Henry Hyde (R-IL) and others have documented how all levels of government have increasingly exploited the power to seize and keep property allegedly involved in the commission of a crime.[13] The abuses are legendary. Authorities have sought to have property worth tens of thousands of dollars forfeited, much of it for minor drug offenses. They have seized valuable property on little more than their personal suspicion that an individual is involved in drug trafficking. Law enforcement agencies have refused to relinquish the confiscated items even when an accused party is not formally indicted for a crime, and even in some instances when a defendant has been acquitted of the alleged crime. Because such forfeiture proceedings can be considered civil rather than criminal trials, the burden of proof for the government is far lower than the requirement of "beyond a reasonable doubt" in criminal cases. Apparently reflecting the attitude that all is fair in war, prosecutors do not seem to mind that they are getting a second shot at an accused based on the absurd fiction that depriving someone of valuable property is not, in a strictly legal sense, "punishment" and, therefore, does not require conviction of a criminal offense.

Abuses of the government's seizure and forfeiture powers have moved far beyond the arena of drug cases. Nevertheless, the drug war has been the principal factor in the malignant expansion of that authority, just as it has been for the lowering of the barriers against

[11]Barbara Whitaker, "A Father Is Fatally Shot by the Police in His Home, and His Family Is Asking Why," *New York Times*, August 28, 1999, p. A7.

[12]For some earlier examples, see Michael Cooper, "Family Says Police Raided Wrong Home," *New York Times*, May 8, 1998, p. A23; Kit R. Roane, "Again, Police in Search of Drugs Raid the Wrong Home," *New York Times*, March 21, 1998; and Timothy Lynch, "Drug War Is Slowly Diluting Constitutional Safeguards," *Los Angeles Daily Journal*, December 2, 1998.

[13]Henry Hyde, *Forfeiting Our Property Rights: Is Your Property Safe from Seizure?* (Washington: Cato Institute, 1995). See also Terrance G. Reed, "American Forfeiture Law: Property Owners Meet the Prosecutor," Cato Institute Policy Analysis no. 179, September 29, 1992.

arbitrary searches. One cannot look at the damage done to the Fourth Amendment without recognizing that the U.S. Constitution has been a major casualty of the war on drugs.

An especially worrisome trend, but an inevitable one, is the increasing militarization of the drug war. Amendments passed in 1981 weakened the provisions of the Posse Comitatus Act that barred the military from involvement in domestic law enforcement. And those amendments were approved specifically to enable the military to assist law enforcement agencies in the enforcement of the drug laws. In the intervening years, the definition of "assist" has grown ever more flexible and expansive.[14]

Proponents of the drug war attempted to draw the U.S. military into the struggle in numerous ways throughout the 1980s and 1990s. In 1988 Congress explicitly directed the National Guard to assist various law enforcement agencies in counternarcotics operations. The following year President George Bush created six regional joint task forces (JTFs) in the Department of Defense to coordinate the activities of the Pentagon and domestic police agencies in antidrug activities. Most ominously, the JTFs were authorized to respond to requests from law enforcement agencies for military reinforcement in drug cases.

To its credit, the military hierarchy has generally tried to resist the pressure for deeper involvement, even though in the immediate post–Cold War period it seemed that the drug war was one of the few missions that might prevent cuts in the Pentagon's budget and the downsizing of its force structure.[15] Leaders of the uniformed services correctly fear that such quasi-police functions are a dangerous diversion from the military's primary role: protecting the American people from foreign military threats. Resistance to calls by the White House for a more extensive role in the fight against drugs led to a surprisingly public tiff between Barry McCaffrey and Secretary of Defense William Cohen in 1997.[16]

[14]Diane Cecilia Weber, "Warrior Cops: The Ominous Growth of Paramilitarism in American Police Departments," Cato Institute Briefing Paper no. 50, August 26, 1999, pp. 3–5.

[15]For a discussion of the attempts during the 1980s to enlist the military as a major participant in both the foreign and domestic phases of the war on drugs, see Ted Galen Carpenter and R. Channing Rouse, "Perilous Panacea: The Military in the Drug War," Cato Institute Policy Analysis no. 128, February 15, 1990.

[16]Bradley Graham, "Drug Control Chief Won't Let Pentagon Just Say No," *Washington Post*, November 24, 1997, p. A17.

Still, the military has been drawn, however reluctantly, into both the domestic and the foreign phases of the nation's drug war. Units of the U.S. Marine Corps began patrolling the border with Mexico in a vain attempt to stem the flood of illegal drugs coming into the United States. The military's comparative advantage—described by one cynic as an unparalleled ability to smash things and kill people—was not well suited for such a delicate mission. In the spring of 1997, a Marine antidrug patrol encountered 18-year-old goat herder Esequiel Hernandez; shots were exchanged and Hernandez ended up dead. Despite a concerted attempt by the military to justify the actions of its troops, the Justice Department finally settled a wrongful death lawsuit with the Hernandez family for $1.9 million.[17]

The tragedy has done little to dissuade drug war advocates from conducting the campaign against drugs as if it were a real war, one in which the military has a central role to play. Just weeks after the Hernandez killing, the House of Representatives voted to station 10,000 troops along the Mexican border to combat drug trafficking.[18] Representative Charles Norwood (R-Ga) remained equally militant a year later, stating "Put the 82nd Airborne on maneuvers down there [at the border] if you want to stop drugs."[19] In the years since the Hernandez incident, National Guard units have been used to raze 42 alleged crack houses in Indiana and to drive drug dealers from open-air markets in Washington, D.C. As law enforcement analyst Diane Cecilia Weber writes, National Guard units "in all 50 states fly across America's landscape in dark green helicopters, wearing camouflage uniforms and armed with machine guns, in search of marijuana fields."[20]

For a nation that once viewed the concept of a standing army with suspicion, the spectacle of military forces—active-duty or National Guard—having a significant domestic presence is more than a little unsettling. But the logic of waging a "war" against the production, sale, and use of certain substances inevitably led to an expanded

---

[17]For a discussion of the Hernandez episode and its implications for the military's participation in the war on drugs, see William Branigin, "Questions on Military Role Fighting Drugs Ricochet from a Deadly Shot," *Washington Post,* June 22, 1997.

[18]Stephen Chapman, "When the War on Drugs Comes Home," *Washington Times,* August 26, 1997, p. A13.

[19]Quoted in "Some Lawmakers Clueless About Life on the Border," *San Antonio Express-News,* May 24, 1998.

[20]Weber, p. 5.

role for the military in that struggle. Symptomatic of the dangerous consequences of viewing drug use as a national security threat was the comment by Attorney General Janet Reno on the occasion of a 1994 technology transfer agreement between the Pentagon and the Justice Department. Reno challenged the military to "turn your skills that served us so well in the Cold War to helping us with the war we're now fighting daily in the streets of our towns and cities across the nation."[21] The point that seemed to elude Reno and others who advocate the militarization of the crusade against illegal drugs is that there is a vast difference between having the military confront enemy armed forces and using similar tactics against American civilians.

Washington's war on drugs has resulted in a growing list of international casualties as well.[22] The prohibitionist strategy has spawned a lucrative black-market trade in several Latin American countries—most notably the Andean nations of Bolivia, Peru, and Colombia. Conservative estimates—including those of the Colombian government—are that illegal drugs amount to between one-quarter and one-third of Colombia's exports, or approximately \$4 billion a year.[23] The lure of massive black market profits, in turn, has produced pervasive corruption and a host of other social dislocations. Although such effects have occurred to some extent in all drug-producing or drug-transiting countries in the Western Hemisphere, they have been the most alarming in Colombia and Mexico.

The situation in Colombia has reached the point where there are now serious doubts about the survivability of the country's democratic system. Marxist rebels, allied with drug-trafficking organizations, now control more than 40 percent of Colombia's territory. They also commit kidnappings, assassinations, and other violent

[21]Quoted in "Technology Transfer From Defense: Concealed Weapon Detection," *National Institute of Justice Journal,* no. 229 (August 1995): 35.

[22]See Ian Vasquez, "The International War on Drugs," *Cato Handbook for Congress— The 106th Congress* (Washington: Cato Institute, 1999), pp. 597–605. Also see Council on Foreign Relations, *Rethinking International Drug Control: New Directions for U.S. Policy* (New York: Council on Foreign Relations, 1997); Kevin Jack Riley, *Snow Job? The War Against International Cocaine* (New Brunswick, N.J.: Transaction, 1996); and Francisco Thoumi, *Political Economy and Illegal Drugs in Colombia* (Boulder, Colo.: Lynne Rienner, 1995).

[23]Larry Rohter, "Colombia Adjusts Economic Figures to Include Its Drug Crops," *New York Times,* June 27, 1999, p. A3.

acts with near impunity even in those areas under the government's nominal control.[24] An increasingly worried U.S. government is now funneling weapons and other aid to the Colombian armed forces, despite evidence of serious human rights abuses committed by some military units. American "advisers" are assisting the military's antidrug efforts inside the country, and rumors continue to circulate that the United States may intervene with its own ground forces if the situation continues to deteriorate.[25]

Even the outside chance of a U.S. military intervention in Colombia to prevent a "Narco-Marxist" regime from coming to power is alarming enough. But even more distressing is that the pattern of pervasive corruption and rising violence convulsing Colombia is being replicated in Mexico.[26] The prospect of similar chaos taking place in America's next-door neighbor is not one that even the most adamant advocates of a noninterventionist foreign policy for the United States could view with indifference.

Calls for Escalation

As victory in the war against illegal drugs remains elusive, the level of frustration on the part of the war's supporters has grown. Frustration, in turn, has led to accusations that the war has not been prosecuted with sufficient vigor and that an even more hardline policy is needed. During the 1992 presidential campaign, Ross Perot contended that, if he were elected, the federal government would

[24]Serge F. Kovaleski, "Rebel Movement on the Rise," *Washington Post*, February 5, 1999, p. A27; Karen DeYoung, "Colombia's U.S. Connection Not Winning Drug War," *Washington Post*, July 16, 1999, p. A1; Larry Rohter, "U.S. Anti-Drug Chief, in Colombia, Speaks of 'Regional Crisis,' " *New York Times*, July 27, 1999, p. A4; and Larry Rohter, "Weave of Drugs and Strife in Colombia," *New York Times*, April 21, 2000, p. A1.

[25]Douglas Farah, "U.S. Ready to Boost Aid to Troubled Colombia," *Washington Post*, August 23, 1999, p. A1; Serge F. Kovaleski, "Colombia Abuzz With Talk of Intervention," *Washington Post*, August 23, 1999, p. A13; and Eric Schmitt, "House Passes Bill to Help Colombia Fight Drug Trade," *New York Times*, March 31, 2000, p. A1.

[26]John Ward Anderson, "Mexican Drug Crisis Echoes Bloody Colombia Pattern," *Washington Post*, August 11, 1997, p. A1; Tim Golden, "U.S. Officials Say Mexican Military Aids Drug Trafficking," *New York Times*, March 26, 1999, p. A1; Tim Golden, "Elite Mexican Drug Officers Said to Be Tied to Traffickers," *New York Times*, September 16, 1998, p. A1; and Douglas Farah, "Drug Corruption in Mexico Called 'Unparalleled,' " *Washington Post*, February 25, 1999, p. A17.

wage a "serious" war on drugs—implying that the ongoing campaign had been half-hearted and ineffectual.

Criticism of that sort burgeoned during the Clinton years. When the president initially sought to scale back the bloated personnel levels of the White House Office of National Drug Control Policy by more than 50 percent, congressional Republicans and other drug warriors reacted with howls of rage and vilification, accusing the president of pursuing a defeatist strategy. Even when Clinton reversed course and sought record funding levels for the federal government's portion of the drug war, the criticism did not abate. Indeed, in the past three years it has actually become more pervasive and vitriolic. Congressional critics have excoriated the administration for not pumping more military aid into Colombia to help the Bogota government combat the insurgency of the Marxist-narco trafficker alliance. (Many of those same Republicans conveniently forget that just a few years ago they were calling for economic sanctions against Colombia and a complete cut-off of military aid because of Bogota's lack of cooperation in Washington's drug war strategy.)

Some of the critics also blame the administration for a modest rise in the percentage of American teens using drugs. Although the substantive features of any alternative strategy—other than a return to the fatuous "just say no" propaganda campaign championed by First Lady Nancy Reagan in the mid-1980s—remain vague, the rhetoric of the critics implies even more dangers to the health of civil liberties in the United States. What is one to make, for example, of Rep. Bill McCollum's criticism of the administration's alleged unwillingness to wage "an all-out drug war"?[27] If the annual expenditure of $16 billion for the federal government's antidrug campaign (plus billions of dollars at the state and local level), filling America's prisons with drug law offenders, and pressuring the governments of drug-producing countries to wage low-intensity conflicts against their own populations are not the characteristics of an "all-out" war, one shudders to contemplate what such hardliners as Perot and McCollum have in mind.

Unfortunately, we have glimpses of what they may have in mind. The uncompromising opposition of pro–drug war forces to even the

[27]Bill McCollum, "Waving the White Flag in Drug War?" *Washington Times,* March 10, 1998, p. A17. Also see "A Timid War on Drugs," editorial, *Washington Times,* December 29, 1997, p. A14.

very modest legislation proffered by Henry Hyde to correct the worst perversions and abuses of the government's seizure and forfeiture powers is one example.[28] For ardent supporters of the drug war the injustice of innocent people being stripped of their property without conviction in a criminal trial is apparently an acceptable price to pay for victory.

Some drug warriors favor even more repressive measures. The most ominous proposal comes from the United Nations. The UN's International Narcotics Control Board's 1997 report called on member states to criminalize opposition to the war on drugs. Citing the 1988 UN Convention Against Illicit Trafficking in Narcotic Drugs and Psychotropic Substances, the INCB claimed that all governments are obligated to enact laws that prohibit "inciting" or "inducing" people to use illegal drugs. If such a vague restriction on freedom of expression were not odious enough, the INCB contends further that member governments are also obligated to ban speech that "shows illicit drug use in a favourable light" or any advocacy of "a change in the drug law."[29] If enacted in the United States, such legislation would, of course, be a flagrant violation of the First Amendment. But it must be remembered that censorship measures—including the banning of opposition to administration policies—have on occasion been a feature of American life during wartime, and received the imprimatur of the courts. It is also not reassuring that the U.S. government has pledged to cooperate with the INCB's global antidrug efforts. Although the Clinton administration did not explicitly endorse the censorship recommendations, neither did it state explicitly that the United States rejects such proposals—even though it certainly could have added that caveat. Indeed, the drug czar's office seems inclined to pursue a mixture of censorship and bribery toward the media. For example, the office reviewed the scripts of popular television programs to determine whether antidrug messages imbedded in the scripts were strong enough to warrant giving the networks credit toward "public service" ads against drugs they were otherwise re-

---

[28]Enactment of forfeiture reform legislation in April 2000 should prevent some—although by no means all—of the abuses committed by law enforcement agencies. Stephen Labaton, "Congress Raises Burden of Proof on Asset Forfeitures," *New York Times,* April 12, 2000, p. A1.

[29]Quoted in Phillip O. Coffin, " A Duty to Censor: UN Officials Want to Crack Down on Drug War Protestors," *Reason,* August–September 1998, p. 54.

quired to run. Such monitoring of speech by a federal agency—
especially when combined with financial inducements upon approval of the content—is more than a little corrosive of the First
Amendment.[30]

The UN bureaucracy is not the only source of intolerance regarding views critical of the war on drugs. Ardent drug warriors have
repeatedly smeared advocates of legalization as constituting a "fifth
column" in the struggle against illicit substances and stated or im-
plied that pro-legalization views are illegitimate. Typical of the
smear tactics was an article by Mary O'Grady, the Americas column
editor at the *Wall Street Journal*, arguing that "American coke-heads"
were guilty of "underwriting" political turmoil and other societal
misery in Colombia.[31] Presidential candidate Steve Forbes and other
supporters of the drug war have similarly argued that proponents
of ballot initiatives legalizing the medical use of marijuana are acting as fronts for the international drug cartels.

When a group of 500 luminaries from around the world—
including Nobel Laureate Milton Friedman, former Secretary of
State George Shultz, and former UN Secretary General Javier Perez
de Cueller—signed a public letter arguing that the global war on
drugs was causing more harm than good and urging that alternatives be considered, the *Wall Street Journal's* editorial page reacted
with a crude smear attempt: "It occurs to us to suggest that the
future of the debate would profit if all of these people stated publicly whether they themselves use any of these drugs recreation-
ally."[32] One can almost hear an echo of the droning question asked
so frequently by Senator Joseph McCarthy: "Are you now, or have
you ever been, a member of the Communist Party?"

Such manifestations of neo-McCarthyism are clearly designed to
silence opposition to the drug war and are unworthy of an honest
debate on an important public policy issue. Unfortunately, it is also
all too typical of a "wartime" mindset in which opponents are seen,
not merely as people who hold a different point of view, but as
traitors to a noble cause.

Those who might be tempted to dismiss the dangers of efforts to

[30]Don Van Natta, "Drug Office Will End Scrutiny of TV Scripts," *New York Times*,
January 20, 2000, p. A11.

[31]Mary Anastasia O'Grady, "American Coke-Heads Underwrite Colombia's Misery," *Wall Street Journal*, August 20, 1999, p. A11.

[32]"500 Drug Geniuses," editorial, *Wall Street Journal*, June 10, 1998, p. A18.

gag proponents of drug legalization should be aware that government officials have already sought to implement censorship measures (albeit more limited ones than the comprehensive bans suggested by some drug warriors). For example, authorities in Maryland prosecuted an individual for publicly divulging the identity of two undercover narcotics officers. Attempting to prohibit such disclosures by charging the defendant with "obstructing and hindering a police officer," Maryland officials endeavored to give undercover narcotics officers the same protection that Congress afforded to CIA and other intelligence agents during the Cold War.[33]

Although the Maryland Court of Special Appeals eventually overturned the conviction on the grounds that it violated the defendant's state and federal constitutional rights to freedom of speech, several aspects of the case remain troubling. First, the fact that Maryland authorities sought to impose such censorship in the first place is worrisome; second, the defendant was convicted at the trial court level; and third, the Court of Appeals decision overturning the conviction was on a divided vote. It is hardly reassuring that even a minority of the justices were willing to allow such a violation of the First Amendment's guarantee of freedom of speech to pass constitutional muster.

Attempts to impose censorship are not the only manifestations of a drive to escalate the war on drugs and use ever more draconian measures. Police officers and other members of outreach programs in the public schools now routinely suggest that students report illegal drug use—by fellow students and even by other family members—to their teachers or other authorities. Rarely do they bother to mention to impressionable youngsters that such revelations could subject parents, siblings, or other relatives to criminal prosecution and possible imprisonment.

Tragically, such incitements to snitch sometimes get the desired result. In September 1999, a 16-year-old Maryland girl turned in her parents to police for growing marijuana in their home. The police promptly arrested both parents and charged them with two felonies and two misdemeanors, and state child protective services officials temporarily stripped the couple of custody of their daughter.[34] Nor

---

[33]That measure was the Agents Identities Protection Act, passed in 1982 following the "outing" of several agents by former CIA agent Philip Agee and the death of one of those agents. For a discussion, see Carpenter, *The Captive Press*, p. 128.

[34]Melissa Healy, "Parents Reach Out to Informant Daughter," *Los Angeles Times*, September 9, 1999, p. A3.

is this an isolated episode. The previous week an 11-year-old Jacksonville, Florida, boy saw his father and stepmother carted off to jail after he reported their indoor marijuana garden to authorities. Earlier in the year, a 16-year-old boy, upset at his family's impending move from New York to Washington, tipped police off about the stash of marijuana in his parents' bedroom. Keith Stroup, executive director of the National Organization for the Reform of Marijuana Laws states that his organization receives at least one call a month from an attorney or defendant whose child has turned in a parent for marijuana use or possession.[35] Since it is unlikely that NORML is informed of every incident—much less those instances in which a child snitched on a family member for using or possessing other drugs—the actual number of cases is undoubtedly larger.

Encouraging in any manner whatsoever children to turn in family members to the police for violating the drug laws has an ugly totalitarian aura. It is reminiscent of similar odious campaigns in the name of ideological conformity in Nazi Germany, the Soviet Union, and Maoist China that Americans once regarded as unique to police states. That it occurs at all in the United States is an alarming indicator of how the concept of a "war" on drugs is warping our society. It has no place in an America that values individual liberties and claims to espouse "family values."

The Expanding Scope of Prohibition

The corrosive consequences of the drug war are not confined to the crusade against narcotics. Perhaps the most insidious effect of the war on drugs is how the American people have become conditioned to think in prohibitionist terms generally. Francis X. Kinney, deputy director for strategy at the Office of National Drug Control Policy, states simply, "Drugs are illegal because they are harmful."[36] But using that standard inevitably puts American policy on a very slippery slope. A good many things are—or at least may be— harmful to their users, including tobacco products, alcoholic beverages, and high-fat foods. If the government can ban certain drugs on that basis, what is the barrier to governmental action to criminalize

[35]Healy.

[36]"It's Time to Rally the Troops in Our War on Drugs," letter to the editor, *Washington Times*, June 20, 1998, p. A14.

those other products? The only barrier would seem to be strong political resistance. Depending on organized resistance for personal protection removes a whole range of behaviors from the arena of choice to the arena of political struggle, where outcomes are anything but certain. Potentially, the rights Americans enjoy today about what substances they put into their bodies could become far more limited in the future.

That is not an excessively alarmist conclusion. After all, most currently illegal drugs were legal earlier in this century. Conversely, America has already had one fling with an attempt by Congress to outlaw alcoholic beverages. No less a drug war luminary than Thomas Constantine, director of the Drug Enforcement Administration, has stated publicly, "When we look down the road, I would say 10, 15, 20 years from now, in a gradual fashion, smoking will probably be outlawed in the United States."[37] The ever-tightening restrictions on the marketing of tobacco products—the banning of billboard advertising; the elimination of vending machine sales; the attempt to bar sales to anyone under 21 years of age; statutes and ordinances prohibiting smoking in restaurants, office buildings, and other "public" locales—all point in that direction.

The situation with respect to alcoholic beverages is not yet as dire, but the assault on the legitimacy of drinking has taken on new vigor in the past six or seven years. (Indeed, one might argue that the alcohol beverage industry is about where the tobacco industry was some two decades ago: beset by annoying but not yet life-threatening restrictions.) The trend, though, is troubling. Under the guise of a campaign against drunk driving, all 18- to 21-year-old Americans have already been stripped of their legal right to drink. Anti-alcohol crusaders are now mounting offensives on several fronts. One of the most significant is the effort to have Congress mandate a nationwide standard declaring that any driver with a blood alcohol level of 0.08 or higher be considered legally drunk. Such a measure passed the Senate and was just narrowly rejected by the House in 1998.

Aside from the fact that the standard itself is draconian (a 100-lb. woman consuming one drink on an empty stomach would find herself at or perilously close to the limit), proponents candidly admit that the .08 mandate would be merely an interim measure. Their

---

[37]"Sex, Drugs and Consenting Adults with John Stossel," ABC News Special Report, May 26, 1998, transcript #98052601-j13, p. 14.

ultimate goal is to ban anyone who has consumed *any* amount of alcohol from driving. Ominously, Karolyn V. Nunnallee, national president of Mothers Against Drunk Driving, notes that "studies show that many people are dangerously impaired at lower levels."[38]

There are indications that the focus on the (admittedly very real) menace of drunk driving is largely a pretext for a much broader attack on the alcohol industry—and even more fundamentally on the legitimacy of drinking such beverages at all. Some of the "anti-drunk driving" measures stretch credulity to the breaking point. For example, the U.S. Senate passed a bill in March 1998 banning *passengers* in a car from drinking. The same measure sought to ban sales entirely from drive-through liquor windows, although senators rejected that provision by a vote of 56 to 43.[39] Similar campaigns are underway at the state and local levels to ban not only such drive-through sales, but even the right of convenience stores and gas stations to sell alcohol.

Reminiscent of the campaigns against tobacco advertising, the advertising of alcoholic beverages has come under increasing fire as well. Some of the criticism is transparently silly—for example the allegation that the Budweiser frogs were a nefarious attempt by Anheuser-Busch to target children as potential consumers. (One wonders what such critics think of the new ad campaign featuring Louie the Lizard and his friend; perhaps lizards have less appeal to children.) Given the tobacco precedent, however, the tendency to smirk at prohibitionist excesses should be resisted. Once again, there is a broad-range attack underway on the right to market an ostensibly legal product.

True, there is no imminent prospect of national legislation outlawing tobacco products and alcoholic beverages. But the same result can be achieved incrementally as well as in a legislative blitzkrieg; it merely takes longer. After all, the great experiment in Prohibition during the 1920s did not occur out of the blue. Indeed, as scholars have shown, the roots of national Prohibition went back more than half a century before the ratification of the 18th Amendment and the enactment of the Volstead Act. And it began innocuously enough, with temperance campaigns to encourage more re-

---

[38]"Americans Are Fed Up with Drunken Drivers," letter to the editor, *Washington Times*, February 5, 1998.

[39]Lance Gay, "Drinking Passengers Hit By Senate Vote," *Washington Times*, March 6, 1998, p. A6.

sponsible drinking or, preferably, voluntary declarations of absti-
nence. The campaign gradually escalated to the passage of local
prohibition ordinances, followed by the enactment of similar laws
on the state level in more and more states. Only then was there a
drive to enact a comprehensive national ban. The tobacco and alcohol industries today face a similar "death by a thousand cuts."

The key point is that the prohibitionist mentality is insatiable by
nature. Once the public accepts the logic that it is appropriate to
outlaw the sale and possession of certain substances (marijuana,
cocaine, and other drugs) because they are "harmful," other substances are vulnerable to attack on that same basis. And who can
dispute the argument that tobacco products and alcoholic beverages
are often harmful to their users? A mountain of scientific evidence
has implicated cigarette smoking as a cause of numerous health
maladies. Similarly, millions of Americans battle alcoholism, and
the effects of that condition impact family members and other innocent parties. Excessive alcohol consumption is a factor in numerous cases of violence as well as other antisocial acts—in addition to
the problem of drunk driving. Indeed, one can make the argument
that alcohol and tobacco cause as many or more societal problems
than do currently illegal drugs. For example, a 1998 study by Columbia University's National Center on Substance Abuse found that
alcohol, more than *any* illegal drug, was closely associated with
violent crimes, including murder, rape, assault, and child and spou-
sal abuse. Twenty-one percent of state inmates convicted of violent
crimes committed them under the influence of alcohol alone, according to the report. Only three percent were high on crack or
powder cocaine and just one percent was under the influence of
heroin.[40]

Proponents of drug legalization often invoke precisely such
points to expose the hypocrisy of the drug war and to call for treating presently illegal drugs the same as tobacco and alcohol. It is
right to point out the flagrant inconsistency of treating various
mind-altering substances in such widely different fashions. But
drug-war opponents should perhaps be more sensitive to the reality
that the inconsistency could be resolved in two ways. One solution
would be to apply the alcohol and tobacco model to illegal drugs.
But the other possibility would be to apply the drug war model to

---

[40]Christopher S. Wren, "Alcohol or Drug Link Seen in 80% of Jailings," *New York Times*, January 9, 1998, p. A11.

alcohol and tobacco.[41] The chances of the second scenario are now at least as great as prospects for the first.[42] Indeed, Gro Harlem Brundtland, the head of the World Health Organization, has virtually declared war on tobacco. She has called for a world-wide ban on all tobacco advertising and for a package of other international controls, including very high levels of taxation.[43] That approach is little more than prohibition on the installment plan.

Downsizing Civil Liberties

The conditioning of the American people to accept whatever is necessary to prosecute the war on drugs creates other dangers in addition to the possibility that a prohibitionist strategy might someday be applied to alcohol and tobacco. The erosion of fundamental civil liberties that began with the drug war is rapidly expanding into other arenas.

For example, just as the courts have lowered the barriers to automobile searches to facilitate police antidrug efforts, the courts have also countenanced such measures as "sobriety checkpoints" (roadblocks) to combat drunk driving and Immigration and Natu-

[41]Critics have correctly pointed out that a prohibitionist strategy—or even a "prohibition-lite" approach of very high taxes on tobacco products—would create (and in some foreign countries already have created) a lucrative black market. See Bruce Bartlett, "Hiking Cigarette Taxes Is Good for (Illegal) Business," *Wall Street Journal*, May 12, 1998, p. A22; Nick Brookes, "Black-Market Bonanza," *Washington Post*, May 20, 1998, p. A25; and Robert Levy, "High Taxes Fuel Black Market," *USA Today*, January 5, 1999.

[42]An especially worrisome development is the growing tendency of prominent drug warriors to link illegal drugs and the two legal products. In a *Washington Post* op-ed arguing that marijuana is a hard drug, former HEW secretary Joseph Califano makes that linkage on several occasions. For instance, in a passage arguing that marijuana was a "gateway" to harder drugs, he adds the observation that "virtually all teens who smoke marijuana also smoke nicotine cigarettes and drink alcohol." He argues that marijuana affects the level of dopamine in the brain, and "may prime the brain to seek substances such as heroin and cocaine that act in a similar way." But then he adds a comment noting that studies have found that nicotine also affects dopamine levels. One must at least consider the possibility that Califano is building the foundation for the case that, not only is marijuana a dangerous drug that must remain outlawed, but that alcohol—and especially cigarettes—must logically be treated the same way. Joseph A. Califano, "Marijuana: It's a Hard Drug," *Washington Post*, September 30, 1997, p. A21.

[43]Betsy Pisik, "WHO Leader Seeks Treaty in Tobacco Fight," *Washington Times*, October 21, 1998, p. A11.

164

ralization Service checkpoints to help apprehend illegal aliens. A colleague of mine encountered such an INS checkpoint on the main highway between San Diego and Los Angeles—some 50 miles from the U.S.-Mexico border—while on his way to a speaking engagement. INS agents (together with members of the California Highway Patrol) pulled cars over—whether randomly or based on some mysterious "profile" was not clear—and interrogated the unlucky motorists. My colleague (who is not Hispanic) was one of those detained. He was asked where he was coming from, what his destination was, if he traveled that route frequently, and what his business was in Los Angeles—as if any of that information was properly the business of INS bureaucrats.

Some Americans (and unfortunately most state and federal courts) have rationalized such intrusions as a "minor inconvenience" that enables law enforcement personnel to pursue a greater good. But it was not that many decades ago that Americans assumed they had a right to drive down the nation's highways and not be molested by authorities conducting investigative fishing expeditions. It would have been considered a revolutionary (and odious) notion that a motorist could be routinely stopped when there was no reasonable cause to believe that he had violated any law. Checkpoints to conduct even cursory interrogations, examine one's papers, or otherwise interfere with one's freedom to travel from place to place were considered the features of dictatorial societies, unacceptable in an America that regarded itself as the citadel of freedom.

Abuses of the government's seizure and forfeiture powers, which had become a hallmark of the drug war, have now expanded into other areas. Authorities in several cities have begun to seize the automobiles of individuals accused of soliciting sex from prostitutes. In early 1999, New York City mayor Rudolph Giuliani expanded the concept still further by ordering the seizure of automobiles of people arrested for drunk driving.

As in the cases of drug war property seizures, valuable property is taken by the authorities upon arrest—before the accused party has been convicted of any crime. The Alice in Wonderland concept of "punishment first, verdict later" seems to have become the operating doctrine of U.S. law enforcement. And as in drug war cases, there is no guarantee that even a "not guilty" verdict will result in the return of property. Mayor Giuliani, in fact, explicitly stated that the city might retain seized property in cases where an acquittal did not seem (to whom?) warranted by the facts.[44] Nor is there any greater protection for the rights of innocent third parties in the new non-drug seizure and forfeiture cases. One key case that went to the U.S. Supreme Court involved a woman who jointly owned an automobile with her husband, who had been arrested for soliciting sex from a prostitute. Although no one disputed the fact that she was in no way involved in the alleged violation of the law (indeed, she was mightily annoyed at her husband), the Court nevertheless upheld the government's seizure and forfeiture actions depriving her of her share (50 percent) of the auto's value.

The drug war has produced other more subtle, but equally dangerous trends. It has led to the militarization of police departments and an increase in the level of force used by police departments in situations that have little or nothing to do with illegal drugs.[45] It has emboldened federal authorities to pursue measures that further dilute the expectation of privacy that customers have when doing business with their bank.[46] Such efforts include the aborted "know your customer" rule proposed by the Federal Desposit Insurance Corporation in early 1999 that would have required banks to know how and where their customers got their money and to monitor accounts to determine whether transactions were "normal." The proposed rule—withdrawn at least temporarily after a storm of public protest—would have greatly expanded the already disturbing requirements that banks spy and report on their own customers.[47]

Although it is possible that such an array of abuses of government power might have become the norm even in the absence of a war on drugs, that is most unlikely. The erosion of key civil liberties coincides with the onset of, or with the incremental escalation of, the drug war. Many insidious practices now becoming pervasive

[44]For a blistering critique of Giuliani's initiative, see Stephen Chapman, "Exceeding Reasonable Limits," *Washington Times,* February 27, 1999, p. D8. See also Alan Finder, "Questions Over City's Plan Against Drunk Drivers," *New York Times,* January 23, 1999, p. A16.

[45]See Weber; and Timothy Egan, "Soldiers of the Drug War Remain on Duty," *New York Times,* March 1, 1999, p. A1.

[46]Joe Davidson, "U.S., in Anti-Drug Move, Plans to Lower Threshold for Money-Transfer Reports," *Wall Street Journal,* May 20, 1997, p. A4; and Richard Rahn, "Treasury's Newest Assault on Privacy," *Investor's Business Daily,* August 12, 1997, p. A28.

[47]Solveig Singleton, "Let Federal Eyes Ogle Your Account?" *Washington Times,* February 10, 1999.

throughout law enforcement either began as features of the drug war or received a huge boost from that struggle. The crusade against drugs has conditioned the American people to listen to the siren song that it is necessary for them to give up a few of their freedoms for the greater good of ridding the nation of the scourge of drugs. Once that rationale is accepted, it becomes ever easier for authorities to use the same argument in the name of combating other "scourges"—such as drunk driving, prostitution, illegal immigration, and the alleged conspiracy by tobacco companies to snare American children.

Adopting a prohibitionist strategy against certain drugs was a bad enough course of action. But using the metaphor of "war" for such a campaign has created an assortment of disasters. Americans now face a fundamental choice: They can end the failed crusade against drugs or they can watch as those disasters burgeon in size and multiply in number.

PART V

A DEBATE: SHOULD AMERICA LEGALIZE DRUGS?

11. Legalization Is the Prudent Thing to Do

Daniel Polsby

The proposition is whether drugs should be legalized. I have been hired to uphold the libertarian side of the argument, which, in a nutshell, treats as suspect uses of the criminal law that are meant to suppress behavior that primarily harms the actor rather than society at large. Ideology alone, however, cannot completely dispose of the question. The practical consequences of legal change, to the extent we can foresee them, count heavily in public policy debate, and we shall find, on close examination, that libertarian arguments might cut in opposite directions in connection with the legalization question.

In order to make it clear what the argument is about, it is necessary to be more specific than usual in identifying the questions that need to be answered. What drugs do we mean? Marijuana is one thing; heroin is another; LSD is yet another; amphetamine yet another; epinephrine yet another. Are all of these drugs to be treated just the same? And what do we mean by "legalized"? Does legalization of a drug mean that it will trade in carefully regulated markets, like prescription medicines? Or in lightly regulated markets, like cigarettes and alcohol? Or in essentially unregulated markets, like M&M's and golf clubs? And if the market is to be regulated in any significant way—for example, children denied access to the commodity—will intentional circumventions of that regulation, or negligent violations of it, be treated as criminal acts? If so, as felonies or misdemeanors?

What drug we're talking about legalizing matters even to a libertarian. Marijuana is, of course, the poster child for legalization. It is a relatively benign substance that imposes modest costs on users and inconsequential costs on the society as a whole. The case for decriminalizing marijuana consumption is strong. But that case is not necessarily readily transferable to other drugs. Many central nervous system stimulants impose more clear-cut health costs on users than marijuana. They are also more socially costly to the extent that they change users' behavior in the direction of edginess and aggression. Drugs like amphetamine would be extraordinarily cheap if they were as legal as golf clubs and their manufacture or distribution involved no legal risk. If drugs are like most commodities, we should expect to see a relationship between declining price and increasing consumption. One can foresee a lot of demand for cheap amphetamine. People often lose weight when they use it; they need less sleep; they do better with boring repetitive tasks (in other words, their jobs). People strung out on amphetamine also become jumpier, more hypertensive, more paranoid, angrier. A world in which amphetamine was as legal and available as M&M's, to take the extreme case, would almost certainly be quite different from the world we live in now, depending upon how much additional drug-taking would follow a meaningful decrease in its price. It might be a nastier and more quarrelsome place. Libertarians ought to care as much as anyone else about this sort of environmental change.

Having to deal with crankheads every day would be only the thin edge of the legalization wedge. Depending on what one meant by "legalization," it might well happen that the market for existing recreational drugs, including cocaine and heroin, would collapse as better and more powerful euphorics, stimulants, anorexics, and narcotics were brought to market, each with its own complement of unforeseeable behavioral side effects. Of course, we do not know what those side effects would be. Nor, for that matter, can we predict how many additional people might eventually develop the drug-taking habit thanks to the reduction in price associated with the removal of the legal risk premium. Accordingly, we cannot know how much in-place social capital would be depreciated or completely torn up by legalization. But it is no use to pretend these perils away. Beyond question, risks can be assigned a negative present value and considered as constituting a present externality.

So far, we have established that there is a basis that should in principle be satisfactory to a libertarian view of the world, upon which coercive regulation of drug consumption might proceed. There are potential externalities that need to be restrained, but there is a further point in favor of regulation for libertarians. This point addresses the large difference between paternalism and self-paternalism. It is one thing for a person to want to regulate someone else's behavior because that other person needs to be controlled for his own good. It is something else again for a person, recognizing his own weakness, to want regulatory restraints for himself. Many people might seek to avoid going anywhere near environments in which drugs were freely available because they fear that, given half a chance, they would impulsively behave in ways not in their own self-interest. Some people cannot, and know they cannot, control themselves in the presence of ice cream; other people cannot, and know they cannot, control themselves in the presence of cocaine. It is not obvious why a libertarian should object if a person should want to take refuge from his own weakness by jiggering the environment in order to minimize temptation—avoiding ice cream parlors or Hollywood parties, for example. Beyond that, it would proliferate different ways of life, and human freedom along with it, if people were free to choose to live not only in the coarse world chock-a-block with drugs and other vices that most of us inhabit, but were also free to choose to live in a different, more benign world—call it the Ward and June Cleaver world—where there were no drugs or other vices, where one could flip on the TV without facing an onslaught of soft-core porn, where gambling and prostitution were frowned on and hidden decently from view. One can have that sort of world with the right kind of laws and law enforcement, which are admittedly coercive. But it is also coercive, a form of interpersonal imperialism to insist that people who want to live in the Ward and June Cleaver world must not by any means be allowed do so, because the preferences of people who want to indulge in vice must always, everywhere, take priority. Maybe it would pay dividends for some nuance to be given to the concept of "legalization," whether of drugs or other vices. It is one thing to say that it should be possible under certain circumstances—some times, some places—for people to indulge in drugs (or other vices) without fear of imprisonment, but something else to say that they ought to be entitled to free access to drugs or other vices at all times and in all places irrespective of how the exercise of this right might affect the environment in which this right is exercised.

The libertarian's theoretical case for legalizing drugs seems to me quite inconclusive, at least if the right to use drugs is framed broadly. As is so often true in life, there are many rights running around in competition with one another and there is no obvious principle that would allow one to assign priority to one and ignore the others. If I were Dan Lungren, I would pitch the case against legalization pretty much that way. Instead, Lungren defends the indefensible, and in the process exposes the most serious, most sober argument for legalizing drugs. It is not an argument rooted in principle but in practice. It is not that some grand moral precept confers a civil right on people to snort their brains out. The better argument is one of prudence rather than one of principle. Experience has shown that attempting to control people's drug consumption through the criminal law is far more costly than it is beneficial. The wonk's First Commandment, that we learned from Guido Calabresi many years ago, is that the aim of public policy ought to be to minimize the sum of (1) the social costs of bad behavior and (2) the costs of enforcement. The costs of enforcement are affected, in part, by the efficacy of enforcement. You could have a given behavior, which was very socially costly, that you might just want to leave alone rather than try to suppress if you thought the costs of suppression were truly stupendous. This is the case with the regulation of drugs through the criminal process.

Dan Lungren defends the war on drugs as though its noble purposes rather than its disastrous effects were the operative datum from the standpoint of social policy. Keeping up this pretense is a remarkable act of self-delusion. Without in any way minimizing the social costs that would undoubtedly flow from legalizing drugs, it is simply incredible to believe that the costs of pursuing the policy of minimizing drug use through the criminal law has not been many, many times more expensive, in treasure, shattered lives, and nasty externalities that have been borne by virtually the entire country.

The dollar costs are the least of it. Of course public budgets directly related to suppression of illegal trade in drugs must be in the range of $30 to $50 billions annually; private budgets are in the hundreds of millions or billions as well. Any number of treaties and international agreements revolve around suppressing the drug trade. Colombia and regions of a number of other countries have become narcocracies. The rents related to the production and distribution of illegal narcotics have made very many bad men very rich. They have used their wealth to corrupt police officers in practically every country in the Western Hemisphere—and many of the incorruptible have been murdered for it. The body count attributable to the war on drugs compares favorably to that of our country's other wars. We know to a reasonable certainty that the now-subsiding murder epidemic of the mid-1980s through early 1990s, which claimed tens of thousands of lives, including thousands of children, was a byproduct of the war on drugs. In the same period

of time, dozens, maybe hundreds of people dropped dead from cocaine overdoses. Let us conservatively assume that in a world of legal
cocaine this body count would be much higher. Even so, it is in-
conceivable that the pharmacological dangers of cocaine could approach in deadliness the collateral damage from the war on drugs.

The violent crime wave that the United States experienced between 1984 and 1992 was unusual in several respects. First, it was
unusual in that a rather sudden spike in the murder rate was em-
bedded in a violent crime rate that had been declining steadily since
the late 1970s. Second—and apparently unprecedented since statistics have been kept—this spike involved an unusual number of
children as perpetrators and as victims. This mini-murder epidemic
was a direct but unintended consequence of prohibitionist drug
laws, just as the violent crime wave of the 1920s was the direct
unintended consequence of the Eighteenth Amendment's prohibition on alcohol.

Scholars have noticed the coincidence between the arrival of crack
cocaine as an important commercial commodity and the spiking of
the rates of murder and victimization among urban males age 14
and older. What happened was a story too complex for policymakers to have foreseen, though its outlines are tolerably clear now, in
hindsight. Crack cocaine, unlike the powdered kind, usually trades
in small batches. A given kilogram of cocaine will yield 10 to 20
times as many retail transactions in the form of crack than it will in
the form of powder. This means that if crack becomes a dominant
product in the cocaine market, that will portend a large expansion
of job opportunities in the retail end of the distribution business.
The war on drugs cannot plausibly be blamed for the development
of the crack cocaine trade, but more or less coincident with the
arrival of crack in the marketplace, the federal government's invest-
ment in the war on drugs nearly sextupled in a matter of only a
dozen years. The war created, transiently, as it turned out, a window of economic opportunity for young men willing to put up with
the rapidly increasing risks, legal and illegal, of drug dealing. Potential competitors abandoned the marketplace, voluntarily or because they were arrested, or, as has apparently happened in many
thousands of cases since the mid-1980s, because they were murdered. Large amounts of cash rewarded those who remained, but
also attracted violence, further diminishing competition and height-
ening the returns in the business. The homicide victimization risks
for African-American males ages 18–24 more than doubled in these

years, to over 100 in 100,000. The criminologist Alfred Blumstein argues that this increase was caused by "the recruitment of young people into illicit drug markets."

This explanation, persuasive as it is so far as it goes, leaves out the second peculiarity of the mini murder epidemic. It does not explain why the victimization experience of *younger* teenagers, whose likelihood of killing or being killed was historically no greater than that of their parents, rapidly increased so as more nearly to resemble that of their older brothers. Why should the war on drugs have sucked in youngsters? What evidently happened was that children too young for the adult justice system began to develop an increasing comparative advantage as drug dealers. During the 1980s there was a rapid inflation, driven by public opinion, in the harshness of the legal system toward adult drug offenders. Meanwhile, the legal risks for juvenile offenders remained relatively constant. One effect of this change was that, as the 1980s progressed, older boys and young men with criminal predispositions found themselves in many cases better off if they substituted robbing drug dealers (whose ranks were beginning to include significant numbers of younger juveniles) for dealing drugs themselves.

In short, changes in the criminal justice system, driven by the war on drugs, simultaneously attracted juveniles into the criminal labor force while making them increasingly attractive targets of criminal predation. The result was deadly. Unless he arms himself with a gun, a fourteen-year-old boy is not usually going to be a match for an eighteen-year-old young man in a violent confrontation. This explains why one should expect to see increased demand by (juvenile) drug dealers for firearms — namely to protect themselves, their inventory, and their receipts from predation by older boys and young men with recently changed legal incentives. And unless he arms himself with a gun, an unarmed eighteen-year-old boy is not usually going to be a match for a fourteen-year-old with a gun. This explains why one should expect to see increased demand for firearms by young adults who prey on younger drug dealers. Blumstein has called this story an "arms race" on city streets. A murder epidemic was the result—an epidemic statistically localized in the urban minorities. The rate of murder for the population as a whole continued its secular, post-1970s' decline; even the rate for the African-American population, apart from the young male cohorts, continued to decline. There is no reasonable explanation of this experience that does not place the blame directly on the war on drugs.

Of course body counts are not the end, indeed are only a bare beginning, of the social costs of the war on drugs. That mini murder epidemic also had an impact on the neighborhoods in which it was occurring, raising the implicit costs of capital for the redevelopment of deteriorated building stock and, in effect, causing some parts of American cities to be abandoned by everyone except those so unlucky and so unresourceful that they couldn't leave. To these costs we should add the tangible and intangible costs of additional regulation—compliance with money laundering laws, increased surveillance of the civilian population by the military and increasingly intrusive law enforcement. To be sure, it was impossible to foresee all these costs when the war on drugs began. But it is easy to see them now. It is worth wondering why, with this record of incredible destructiveness on the books for all to see, defenders of the status quo like Dan Lungren continue to press the argument about drug legalization versus criminalization as though it were about the question whether it is a good thing or a bad thing for someone to become a dope addict.

12. Legalization Would Be a Mistake

Daniel Lungren

I am not a libertarian. I realize there are libertarian strains in the conservative movement, but I consider myself a *conservative*, which means I am dedicated to a society of ordered liberty. That is a society dedicated to freedom with responsibility, not unfettered freedom. It is a society that understands that there are some limits to freedom. Therefore, the question for politicians, supposedly people elected to make tough public policy decisions is, Where do you draw the line? The questions that must be addressed regarding policy are these: (1) Has the line been drawn in the wrong place? (2) Is the war on drugs a failure? (3) Is it such a failure that we need to get rid of it?

There are several directions that such a debate can take. For instance, if you are dedicated to the idea of unfettered freedom and liberty and you believe either that using drugs has no negative social effects, or if it does have negative social effects they are outweighed by your dedication to unfettered freedom, then in fact you do not care about the consequences of changing our approach to drugs. To you, the question of possible deleterious effects or even those suggested by Professor Dan Polsby would not even be instructive, much less persuasive.

There are those who argue that, while there are negative impacts on society of drug use, nonetheless the approach that we are now taking is unsuccessful. For them the argument registers on different levels. There is the economic model: What are the costs? I have heard Professor Polsby talk about the "social cost." I always worry when people talk about social cost. I talk about human beings, flesh and blood human beings. I talk about mothers and fathers and brothers and sisters. I talk about people in my generation whose lives were ruined by the drug scourge of the 1960s when we had de facto decriminalization of drugs in terms of attitude. I saw the lives

179

of too many people of my generation ruined by the lure of drugs and by a society that urged them to "go ahead and use it; if it feels good do it." Some people from my high school and college are still wandering the streets, their minds dulled by drug use.

I suppose some will say that that is just one of the breaks in a free society. We will always have those among us who submit to temptation. I would argue that a society dedicated to ordered liberty has an obligation to investigate whether the policies it implements through its laws encourage or discourage such conduct. Do we have an obligation to assist people? Yes, at times. People sometimes need assists in life, particularly young people. It seems to me the mark of a mature society is that as adults we are willing to give up some things in the interest of our children. That is not a libertarian thought, but I believe that is a thought appropriate to an ordered society. It is part of the obligation we have to the younger generation.

Therefore, I look upon the question posed by this debate in part as what the impact would be on the young people of America. We are informed by prior experience. For example, we had a de facto legalization of marijuana in Alaska, as a result of a ruling by the Supreme Court of Alaska interpreting the right of privacy in its constitution. Basically it decriminalized marijuana for private use by adults. A doubling of the use of marijuana by young people in Alaska followed almost immediately. And it remained at twice the level of marijuana use by young people the same age in the rest of the country.

Now some suggest marijuana is not harmful and that we should not worry about it. But I do worry about it, particularly in terms of its impact on young people. One of the difficulties of life is getting through adolescence; it is part of the maturing process. You are met with setbacks. You are met with failures. You are met with obstacles. And you have to work through that. Marijuana has the effect, when used by young people, of not letting them confront those problems. It interferes with the maturing process. It is a serious question, one that I continue to take seriously even though I am no longer an elected official or the chief law enforcement officer of my home state.

I know that the burden of proof lies with those who would change the law. I don't think that you can argue against the fact that the costs in homelessness, unemployment, welfare, lost productivity, disability payments, school dropouts, lawsuits, medical care costs, chronic mental illness, accidents, crime, child abuse, and child neglect would all increase if we in fact legalized drugs. Perhaps some of you may say it's worth it in the pursuit of unfettered freedom. If that's your position I can understand your sincerity. But I would argue against such results for our society. Even Professor Polsby admitted that with legalization drug use would be more pervasive in our society. One of the questions I asked Governor Johnson was "Do you think that drug use is positive, negative, or socially and morally neutral?" Now for those who think that it is socially and morally neutral I can see why you would suggest, "well there's no problem. So we have more use. That's just one of the decisions people make." But if you believe that drug use of the kind we are talking about leads to destructive behavior, leads to widespread increases in social problems, then you have to ask yourself a question: Is it worth it? Can we afford it?

There are those who focus on the cost-effectiveness of the drug war. When people ask, "Has the war on drugs been a success or a failure?" I say, "It depends on when you're talking about it. It depends on what part of it you are talking about." When I was in Congress in the 1980s I supported the 1984 Comprehensive Crime Control Act and I was one of the chief authors of the '86 and '88 drug laws. And I stand proudly by them, although I would be happy to revisit any aspect of them that critics think should be changed. I can recall, for instance, a meeting that I had when the penalties for crack cocaine were increased. One liberal Democrat expressed some concerns by people in the minority community in his district. They had told him, "This is killing our people. Change the laws so that we can recover our communities." That's the reason for the increase in penalties for crack cocaine. If people now say it has proven over the last 10 or 15 years to be disproportionate, let's review it. But by and large I remain supportive of those laws that I authored, backed, and voted for.

In the 1980s we saw a reduction in drug use in this country. Every survey shows it among both adults and young people. We saw a 50 percent decrease in drug use by those of high-school age. Then at the beginning of the 1990s we saw a doubling of drug use, particularly marijuana, by people of high-school age. We waged a war on drugs in both decades, so what happened? The war on drugs we had in the 1980s was a consistent policy package. True, it may have gone under the rubric of Nancy Reagan's "just say no" campaign, but it was more than that. The particular philosophy encapsulated by that slogan was consistent from top to bottom. There was no question about it. Some of us talked with the folks in Hollywood and we said, "You are glamorizing drug use. You are embarrassing yourself and harming the country." And Hollywood got rid of its glamorization of drugs and actually assisted with some public service announcements and did other things to help deglamorize drugs.

But what happened at the beginning of the '90s? Hollywood fell off the wagon. They began once again to permit the glamorization of drug use. Worse than that, they were again absent from the activity of creating antidrug messages. From top to bottom the message was, "Hey, its not that important." Budgets were cut. We elected a president who kind of laughed about it. When asked about marijuana use, he chuckled and said, "Well if I had another chance I'd try it again because you know I tried it once." To me that was an embarrassment. The message was very clear: "What we said in the '80s really isn't true. It's not that bad; why don't you try it?" And a lot of kids did. As a result, we experienced a doubling of marijuana use in the first six years of that administration. Thank God now we have seen a leveling off.

In the 1980s we got the private sector to become involved in the antidrug effort; now the private sector wants to stay there. Why? Because they have seen that they have fewer days off from their workers, less disability, greater productivity, and fewer problems at the work site because fewer and fewer people are drugged out or influenced by drugs at the work site. Maybe some are proud of the fact that prior to our effort in the 1980s we were known as the most drugged society in Western civilization. I wasn't. I was embarrassed by it. And when you look at our opportunity to participate in the international marketplace, competing with other countries, do you really think having a drugged-out society is going to enable us to compete.

I think some people who support the position that I take make a big mistake when they say, "What we've done in the past, everything's absolutely right. I'm not going to look at anything. I'm not going to see if we ought to fine-tune things." I think they're wrong. We should always be ready to re-examine our positions. But in terms of the proposition presented that we ought to reverse our field and instead of having an antidrug campaign with antidrug laws, we ought to move toward legalizing drugs, I think that the impact on us as a society is just too great.

I am 53 years of age. I graduated from high school in California in

'64 and from college in '68. That was just the beginning of the big drug culture, particularly in California. Do you remember what it was like? Do you really remember what it was like? Oh, hell yes, some of you may say; it was a lot of fun. But that is a strange definition of fun. I recall the high percentage of our folks in our armed forces who were addicted to heroin. There was a huge percentage of people on drugs on a regular basis in the armed forces. And what did we do in response? We turned it around with a strong zero-tolerance program; we eliminated drug use by and large in the military. It worked. So now I would ask you, "Do you want to have people with badges running around in our police departments on drugs? Do you want to be flying in an aircraft with a pilot on drugs who just smoked a joint to try to relieve his tension?" I think you have to say, "I recognize that there is an impact on the ability of someone to think, to respond to situations, to be involved in the world." And that's what we're really talking about.

So I would argue that we cannot afford to change our overall approach, even as we revisit parts of it to see if we need to fine-tune them. The reality is that the social and fiscal costs—however you want to define them—would be greater with a reversal in our overall approach than they are now. Don't think for a moment that changing the policy will result in a net savings of money. I think the result would be a net increase in money. Even if that were not the case, it would result in destructive activity in the lives of human beings in this society that we cannot afford.

Contributors

Ted Galen Carpenter is vice president for defense and foreign policy studies at the Cato Institute.

Steven Duke is professor of law at Yale University.

Gary E. Johnson is governor of New Mexico.

David Klinger is professor of criminology at the University of Missouri.

David B. Kopel is director of research at the Independence Institute.

Michael Levine is a former agent of the Drug Enforcement Agency.

Daniel Lungren is a former attorney general of California.

Timothy Lynch is director of the Cato Institute's Project on Criminal Justice.

Joseph D. McNamara is a research fellow at the Hoover Institution.

Roger Pilon is vice president for legal affairs at the Cato Institute.

Daniel Polsby is associate dean for academic affairs and professor of law at George Mason University.

Julie Stewart is president of Families Against Mandatory Minimums.

Index

Cato Institute

Founded in 1977, the Cato Institute is a public policy research foundation dedicated to broadening the parameters of policy debate to allow consideration of more options that are consistent with the traditional American principles of limited government, individual liberty, and peace. To that end, the Institute strives to achieve greater involvement of the intelligent, concerned lay public in questions of policy and the proper role of government.

The Institute is named for *Cato's Letters*, libertarian pamphlets that were widely read in the American Colonies in the early 18th century and played a major role in laying the philosophical foundation for the American Revolution.

Despite the achievement of the nation's Founders, today virtually no aspect of life is free from government encroachment. A pervasive intolerance for individual rights is shown by government's arbitrary intrusions into private economic transactions and its disregard for civil liberties.

To counter that trend, the Cato Institute undertakes an extensive publications program that addresses the complete spectrum of policy issues. Books, monographs, and shorter studies are commissioned to examine the federal budget, Social Security, regulation, military spending, international trade, and myriad other issues. Major policy conferences are held throughout the year, from which papers are published thrice yearly in the *Cato Journal*. The Institute also publishes the quarterly magazine *Regulation*.

In order to maintain its independence, the Cato Institute accepts no government funding. Contributions are received from foundations, corporations, and individuals, and other revenue is generated from the sale of publications. The Institute is a nonprofit, tax-exempt, educational foundation under Section 501(c)3 of the Internal Revenue Code.

CATO INSTITUTE
1000 Massachusetts Ave., N.W.
Washington, D.C. 20001